The Goldfish That Jumped

First published in the United Kingdom by
Porto Publishing May 2011

Porto Publishing
59 The Avenue
Ealing
London
W13 8JR
UK

www.portopublishing.com

A CIP catalogue record for this book is available from the
British Library, London.

Design and Layout by Porto Publishing

Cover Design by Mark Rigby
info@studio5creative.co.uk

Cover Images:
Irina Tischenko - Goldfish
Charlie Bishop - Kingfisher

ISBN 13: 978-1-905930-03-6

Paper used in the production of this book complies with the following:
UK - Forest Stewardship Council™ (FSC®) certified.
USA - Sustainable Forestry Initiative® (SFI®) certified

PORTO
PUBLISHING
LONDON UK

The Goldfish That Jumped

Mary Curtis

PORTO
PUBLISHING
LONDON UK

Contents

Foreword - My Inner Journey   vii

Testimonials   ix

Acknowledgements   xi

Introduction   1

Chapters

Twice Christened   7

Trust   11

The Loneliness of Crowds   15

The Light Inside the Darkness   21

Living.   25

The Early Years   27

Realisation of Truth.   51

Rebirth   55

The World Through My Eyes   59

The Simplicity of Nurturing   61

This Was All About Me   63

Let The Magic Begin   67

Rebirth (Again)   71

New Beginnings & Castlerigg   75

Jet Propulsion   79

The Wow Factor   83

The Journey Continues   87

More Jigsaw Pieces   89

Deepening Wisdom   93

The Power and Memory of Water   97

Manifestation Work   101

A Deepening of Respect   103

$e = mc^2$ 107

Moving On   113
Be Careful What You Wish For   115
Fast Track Learning   117
A Little Diversion   119
A Little Light of Hope at the End of the Tunnel   125
A Lesson in Trusting Myself   127
New Lessons   133
Deja Vu   137
A New Home   143
New Beginnings   145
Illusions   149
Expect the Unexpected   151
Back to Business   161
The First Stage of Hell   171
The Second Stage of Hell   175
Moving On (Again)   177
Friendships Through Lifetimes   181
Nearing Completion   201
Cae Mabon   205
Coincidence? – Definitely Not!!   209
Limitlessness   211
Following my Heart and Soul   215
Meditations   217
Glastonbury and Chalice Well   221
Hawaiian Huna Healing   229
Music   243
The Present Present   245

Bibliography   251

Author Information   255
Merchandise   257

Foreword

My Inner Journey

"The Soul walks not upon a line,
neither does it grow like a reed.

The Soul unfolds itself,
like a lotus of countless petals."

Kahlil Gibran

Mary Curtis was born with exceptional gifts of psychic awareness and has been balancing energies from as far back as she can recall. She now works as a psychic, clairvoyant, medium, healer & teacher. She is also a homeopath and hypnotherapist. Although working predominantly in the U.K. she has also worked briefly abroad. She has a huge client base, having had many miracles with patients and clients alike. Her success rate is over 97%, patients usually feeling the difference after only one treatment.

Her personality is loving and compassionate. There is a sense of peace and tranquillity around her that is second to none, something I have rarely experienced. There is no sense of judgement around this special lady and being in her presence is a very wonderful, pleasurable experience.

Merely by meeting her and being in her presence, healing begins to take place, and miracles can occur within the quiet sanctity of her simple, candle lit healing room.

She has written this book with love and compassion; to share with you a story that has been germinating in her mind for over eight years. Her spiritual journey takes place over a decade of personal development, looking within and learning about who she is and why she is currently here on Earth.

It's a voyage of self-discovery and at times raw honesty. It is her sincere wish that you enjoy the book, take something from it and glean a different perspective and sense of personal understanding of your own soul.

She hopes the book will indeed touch your soul and assist you in becoming all that you want to be. Several of her friends read the book in its early stage and were extremely kind, making suggestions and alterations. Just at a time when she herself doubted it would be finished they provided their inspiration and support. Her heart-felt thanks goes to each and every one of them, many times over.

Note: Usage of the phrase 'déjà vu' – is used throughout the book to denote a Past Life déjà vu, not merely a déjà vu from this current lifetime.

Catherine Delaney

Testimonials

Thank you so much for the review copy of your book. I couldn't stop reading it!

I finished it at 1:00 am this morning!! It is fantastic Mary, it just goes to prove even more what I already thought, what a truly special, wonderful and amazing woman you are.

I had been feeling run down again but your book has turned me around today, and given me such inspiration to achieve what I want. I am positive the book will be a best seller and can only begin to imagine what wonders you have to come!

I am planning in a few weeks to start attending your meditation classes....

Lots of love   Sian xx

A real page turner. It made me laugh, cry, rejoice, grieve and all of them at once.

Marian Dunn

A book not to be missed, finished reading it on Monday and it is a book that leads you from one chapter to the next in awe of someone who has worked through her life's challenges, which are more than most people would want to experience, and ties in spiritual learning and awakening that we can all share and take into our own lives.

Kevin Webster

A book of real courage and determination, brilliant, I have been inspired and deeply touched

Eamonn Mgherbi
Games & Film Industry Director

A fab book by a tenacious, awesome and heart centred authoress learning to trust in her abilities, life and the universe, whilst empowering others to do the same bringing their gifts to this lifetime.

Can't wait for the published version and the sequel! Hugs

Sara Hayselden

A true "Hero's Journey"!

Kate Trafford

Wow Mary, what a magnificent work, from the heart and journey of real life experience towards your destiny - profound insights to life that I can really learn from.

PianomanTim Gb

I am full of admiration for your achievement in writing it, and the way you have totally turned your life around. It's inspirational and very encouraging and I hope that I will be buying a signed copy from you before too long!

Love and blessings Rachel

Compelling, powerful, triumphant, fast-paced – cleverly weaves important life lessons for all of us into an irresistible story that demands to be read.

Christine Miller
Founder Editor & CEO, Your Ultimate ReSource

…gives the reader a glimpse of what it is like to have the ability to see and feel the energies of others. It is great to know there are others out there who understand heightened sensitivity, because we can often feel alone… written by a healer to reach out to those who need guidance and compassion.

Eric C. Chance
Author

Acknowledgements

I dedicate this book to those who have touched
my life and helped re-awaken my soul.
For all who have encouraged me and given me
unconditional love and support.

To my most dear family, my sons, daughters
and granddaughters. Special hugs to Diane for
teaching me Reiki healing many years ago...
what a journey you started.

My dearest friends Julie, Bev, Cassie, Catherine,
Dennis, Russell, Mark, Marion, Barry, Pat,
Geoff, Neil, Claire, Molly, Sara and Dave, Greg
and Kate, Anapaula, Jennifer, Dorothy, Bernard
and Kerry. Special thanks to all the meditiation
group too, sincerest thanks for supporting me
when otherwise I might have given up. To all
those in the spirit world, my guides, Ascended
Masters and power animals.

My most special and deepest heartfelt thanks
goes to Kevin, my absolute rock, best friend,
twin-flame and souls' companion. I love
you more and more every day. May we be
blessed each day with precious time to
spend together and BE.

My love goes to you all

Introduction

What You as the Reader can Expect From This Book

I have been blessed to inspire and heal many people in my life so far. Some of these stories may seem far reached, extraordinary and miraculous. I assure you that they are all true.

These are all miracles that I have facilitated after jumping from the Goldfish bowl. If you feel that your life is like swimming around and around then you know at some inner level, you may just realise after reading this book that you too have the power within to change your life, there is more to you than you realise.

'The goldfish had to jump out of the bowl' she mused, 'I felt lost as if I was swimming round and round in circles', every day felt the same, and deep within I had this gnawing feeling that there was something more to life that I had to discover. But what? I had no clue. I was a civil servant in a failing marriage with 4 kids, little money, and no future. Something had to change, but how?

I was scared, terrified in fact. My mind was on an overdrive of worry. Should I stay in a belittling failing marriage for the sake of the children? Could I manage on my own? Would they be split up or taken away from me all together?

What seemed impossible back then, against all the odds, has actually come to pass. Through my awakening and faith in spirit, I now have four beautiful, normal, well adjusted young adult children successfully making their way in the world. I have a thriving holistic practice and a deep passion for my work. I love my 'job' and wake up every morning looking forward to my day.

This is my story, but it could be your story too. If you feel like the world is too difficult or not what you want it to be, then take this book home with you and let me hold your hand on your journey, use my words, life story and experiences to give yourself the courage to step forth and dare to be the person you always wanted to be.

Let the book ignite your soul's flame. What gifts and skills are lying dormant within you? What lies deep within your heart? What I discovered within me was the healer, the teacher and the psychic. You may have these gifts or some other gifts; you may be a highly skilled artist, sculptor, musician, singer, farmer, police officer, accountant, warrior, organiser or domestic goddess/carer. As I take you on my inner journey, let me help you to find yours.

By following the steps I took to find my inner self, you can find your stepping stones and release your inner power. These may already exist within you, they just need fine tuning. Perhaps you feel there is something more to life and need to find courage.

The initial step is to look at your life honestly. Are you happy? We often focus on what we haven't got, rather than being grateful for all the things we actually do have in our life. What would you like to introduce into your life? How well do you cope with change? Two things we can be sure of in life are death & change.

2

Once you begin to be aware of what is around you, the fog begins to clear and usually we feel we know, or connect more with our life purpose/destiny. Developing an awareness of The Law of Attraction, we begin to see and understand that we have manifested all of our life's experiences. We then begin a journey into personal responsibility.

We awaken from a deep sleep of blame and influence of outside circumstances, eventually realising that we are in control of our destiny and, in fact always were!

Life changing events can begin in the smallest of ways. Let me just give you a few highlights that I will expand upon as we go through the journey, within these pages.

Daniel is a well-known opera singer. He had lost his ability to sing and had been through the conventional medicine system, having had numerous tests, many of the results of which were contradictory. This had all had a financial impact and his bank account was several thousand pounds lighter.

He called me when he was at a point of despair in his life. Singing opera was his passion which had suddenly been taken from him. Following one healing his voice returned, within four sessions, he was on top note, pardon the pun! He is now able to perform whenever he chooses and his passion for life has now returned, especially now he has married his soul companion who just so happens to be a close friend of mine too.

YOU CAN DO THIS – WHEN WILL YOUR INNER GOLDFISH JUMP? WHAT ARE YOU WAITING FOR?

Equestrian healing is another string to my bow. One Friday afternoon I received a phone call from a young lady who was very distraught whilst she explained that her friends' horse had a suspected brain tumour and the vet had advised that he be put to sleep. He was unable to bend his head down to reach his food and was could not walk. Previously his owner had won awards as he was a show horse.

They had been given six days to make a decision. Her enquiry was as to whether or not healing would be an option. I obviously advised that it would indeed be suitable and, whilst on the telephone could feel the healing energy. I felt a magical connection with the horse instantly.

My diary was rather busy and the earliest opportunity I had would be to squeeze in a visit to see him that Sunday morning, before attending a wedding. In the meantime, I was sending healing continuously to him, and, by the time I saw him, he was already able to bend his head to his food. As I placed my healing hands on him and he gladly accepted the magic.

Throughout the session, he kept bending his head lower and lower. It was as though he was proving that it was working for him. His owner had explained that since the phone call on Friday afternoon there had been a rapid improvement. I returned again on Tuesday as, by this time, only two days remained until the vet's pending decision.

His owner had arranged for photographs to be taken of him as memoirs the following day. She had been distraught and it was very concerning for her that her beautiful pet may have to be destroyed. It seemed life was in the balance. After the session, his health improved considerably.

The vet reassessed him two days later and was incredulous. However, despite this improvement, the vet was still not convinced that he would ever return to full fitness. His decision was that he would not walk again, nor be ridden again and certainly would never be fit enough to enter and win competitions. Within months he was proven wrong and I am pleased to say that it was a great privilege to be a part of his full and speedy recovery.

Another success was that with a farmer who had ulcerated eyes. His eyes produced no tears and they were extremely painful, red and sore. He was being treated by the hospital and had suffered from the effects of the medication and methods of diagnosis and treatment. When he asked me to help I explained that I would do my best and was glad to help. His eyes began to water with one healing and he made a full recovery that day.

Several patients have received healings for infertility, as a result of healings, one patient had twins, another a little boy and another patient now has a beautiful daughter.

Alexandria is a very dear friend. As an estate agent, it was her job to show potential viewers around properties. On one such occasion she had broken her foot. Despite having had the foot in a cast, she was still in a lot of pain several weeks later and was disappointed as she had been looking forward to a skiing holiday. This now seemed out of the question. Following one healing she could hardly believe how much stronger the ankle was, and, indeed, she managed to thoroughly enjoy the skiing holiday.

There are many stories like this. Patients who come with complaints that conventional medicine cannot treat nor cure. I have treated sarcoidosis, lung problems, post-operative complaints, rheumatoid arthritis, to name but few.

Mary Curtis

The Goldfish That Jumped

Twice Christened

*Open your eyes to see, your ears to listen
and your heart to feel.*

"Silence is Golden" was the one of the best selling singles when I was born in 1967. Someone was having a laugh! I am certainly not a party animal and I really love and welcome silence; but I am here on a spiritual journey embracing communication. So, here is my first book. I sincerely hope you enjoy it – whether it brings a tear to your eye, a smile to your face or joy to your soul. Maybe it will do all three.

My date of birth is 4th June, making me a Gemini; known for the connection to Mercury and its relevant communication skills. This book has certainly made me look, honour and cherish those skills to their maximum capacity. Enjoy.

I was the first born child of three children. Like all pregnant women, mum attended the ante-natal classes frequently and was very disappointed when I still hadn't arrived on the due date. The clinic was located about three miles away from her home. As she did not drive, it was a very long walk for a heavily pregnant lady.

Waddling whilst walking with swollen ankles into Leyland town centre was a real challenge for her. My expected date of delivery was mid May, many babies are born early and, like all new mothers, mum was hoping to hold me earlier than the due date. Mid May arrived and there was still no sign of her firstborn. She was growing ever bigger and ever more frustrated too. Week after week she trudged into the town centre, only able to wear loose fitting sandals, on her ever swelling feet. The doctors and nurses checked her out and sent her home again.

All the baby ware; pram, cot, and nappies, were to hand. Yet, week after week there was no sign of the guest of honour at the party. The frustration built up daily.

A normal full-term pregnancy lasts 40 weeks and for any prospective mother, the last few weeks are a time of patience and unrest, as I can attest myself, four times! With baby-bag ready two weeks earlier, all are on tenterhooks, waiting for the slightest sign of baby arriving imminently. Each and every twinge or pain is checked and double-checked as the onset of labour is both exciting and the holds the scariness of the unknown.

The medical profession now recognise that the placenta stops working in the 40th week of a pregnancy. This is why babies are often induced if the labour hasn't commenced within ten days of the due date. Overdue mothers are closely monitored as the baby's welfare is at high risk at these times, and my mother had many of the classic symptoms of high blood-pressure; pre-eclampsia, an extremely dangerous, potentially fatal condition for both mother and baby.

It was now the beginning of June. Her pains started and she was taken to Chorley hospital. She was told to walk in the grounds and left to her own devices. The pains became more frequent though still there was no sign of me. Eventually she was placed in a side ward which meant she felt very secluded from the other women. Almost 60 hours had passed; she was frustrated and exhausted as she was wheeled into the labour ward.

By now it was the 4th June; her prolonged labour had caused foetal distress. The only hope of my survival was the decision that she would have to have a Caesarean section. An ambulance was organised and she was rushed from Chorley Hospital to Preston Royal Infirmary. She was quickly anaesthetised as the staff raced to save us both.

At 3am on Sunday 4th June 1967, I eventually appeared, three weeks later than I had been due: making a surprise entrance into the world, as a very much alive baby, the midwives were astounded as there was NO placenta left. They said it was an absolute miracle that I had survived.

The doctors immediately discovered I had a heart murmur and I was instantly whisked off to an incubator. As mum was coming around from the experience she was told of the seriousness of my condition, it was very unlikely that I would survive for more than a few hours. She was not allowed to hold me and had not even had a chance to touch her new baby. She was advised to have me baptised immediately.

This was very serious. Imagine the despair she felt; not to mention the pain and anguish, the exhaustion and the hell of a 60 hour labour only then to be cut open under the surgeon's knife, a very rare surgery back in those days, with even less communication from the doctors? It must have been awful, particularly when she was advised that my health was still so poor it was suggested that I be baptised again!

All pregnant women look forward to the day they take their baby home, show the baby to friends and family and have the joy of watching that child grow up. All hopes and expectations were dashed. For two days, she wasn't allowed to see me. To even try to comprehend that all the emotional pain, mental anguish, physical pain and endurance were seemingly for nothing.

Mum recalls getting home from the hospital and seeing the empty pram and bursting into floods of tears. Throughout the pregnancy she had looked forward to walking with me and her mum through the local park, now her hopes were dashed.

The Goldfish That Jumped

Mum said she had so wanted to take me home and show me off to her friends and family. For almost a week, she sat, worried, nervous, anxious, popping round to my Gran's but not being able to sit still, and still in pain from having her stomach muscles deeply cut. Finally, the message came from the hospital and my Dad rushed my Mum to the Children's Ward of Preston Royal Infirmary. At last she could hold me, was able to take me home and could enjoy looking after her new baby.

Trust

"The goal is to be an instrument of God.
The more confident we are,
the more our intuition works through us

Paul Neary

So, I had made quite a dramatic entrance into the world. Will it be as dramatic when I leave? For now I am concentrating on "being". Enjoying my life and participating in what I enjoy doing the most. The simplest of pleasures to me is spending time with partner, friends and family. As many of us do, I particularly love being with my granddaughters. Their laughter and sense of fun keep me youthful and inspire me too.

Have you ever felt as though you have known someone for years upon the initial meeting? Have you ever had a knowing that "something" was wrong? Ever felt that a business idea was just right, absolutely and would be a wonderful venture? Ever known that a holiday would change your life?

Maybe that someone wasn't just ill but really poorly? Ever known something was about to happen? Ever heard of others doing the same or the power of miracles? Ever met a child and thought there is a wise old sage there in that little body?

By trusting your intuition this becomes more and more part of everyday life. By accepting and welcoming our intuition, by listening carefully and interpreting clearly what we feel, we can develop this sense of knowing and, just as exercise makes us stronger, so the more you use intuition, the more it strength it gathers.

The more strength it gathers so the more your soul develops and the more aware you become – both of yourself and those around you. You begin to understand when something is absolutely right, when you need to be somewhere and, indeed, who you need to be with too.

You begin to go with the flow of life much more easily, have an acceptance of the bigger picture and a knowing that everything happens at the right time and place. You usually feel you are more in contact with Source/God/The Universe. You become more insightful about what you want in life and who you want to be around, friends, loved ones and family.

The more you learn to accept and understand yourself, so the more you learn to accept and understand others. As this spiritual shift deepens you learn more and more about yourself. All previous experiences have shaped you into the person you are today.

Often we learn how NOT to be from the people most close to us. How many times have children been treated cruelly by their parents yet then go on and become a wonderful, kind, loving parents themselves?

Dave Pelzer in his book "A Child Called It" is a prime example of this: He moved from having been beaten, starved and treated with so much cruelty and neglect that he eventually changed his life around. Despite the intense emotional despair, he always knew that something would improve. His books are testimony to the strength of spirit and also to the fact that, very often we grow in spiritual strength from what can often be our darkest moments.

As Dave shares his personal story, he takes you on a journey of his self-discovery. He had huge trust issues and the only way he could deal with them was to relive and eventually accept his learning from them. The strength and endurance of this man is incredible. We all have the potential to succeed in life though often we get caught up in the drama of the situation becoming distracted from The Truth.

Dave Pelzer is now a well respected author and lectures across the globe. He provides understanding, hope and inspiration to thousands of people. We all have a story to tell and one that can inspire others should they wish to take that lead.

The Souls Truth lies within each and every one of us. It is for us to find our deepest inner self and fulfil our life purpose, by following our hearts and learning to BE. There are many other authors who write about their deeper understanding and acceptance of all that is within this world.

As my friend Dennis states, "Go within, or go without". By going within our souls, we begin a journey into understanding all that has influenced us and what makes us what and who we are today. We have all experienced darker times and by understanding and taking personal awareness and responsibility then we can experience a feeling of a soul to soul deepening within these learning curves. This is my story of unfolding and development, I hope you enjoy and are inspired by it.

I have always trusted and usually been able to interpret my intuition, learning more and more about this from my earliest years. Even as a child I had a wealth of knowing before the age of five. I now realise that this knowing comes from the soul. As a very young child I was aware that I was different.

My awareness and deep inner knowing showed me just how different I was. Often I felt I did not belong on Earth and had a knowing of other planets and civilizations too. I had no explanation for these feelings and knowing at the time – I just accepted that I knew. It was an uncomfortable concept, I frequently felt like a fish out of water, yet was not able to fully comprehend how I felt, nor had I then, the emotional maturity to be able to explain my feelings to others.

The Goldfish That Jumped

The Loneliness of Crowds

"I am me. In all the world there is no one else
exactly like me. There are persons like me,
but no-one who adds up exactly like me.
Therefore everything that comes out of me is
authentically mine because I alone chose it."

Virginia Satir

Looking back I still remember that feeling of aloneness. I felt totally separated, as I was aware that others didn't see, hear or feel, or experience, what I did. This meant I had no-one to talk to, no-one with whom I could discuss my feelings and no-one with whom I could discuss what I saw, heard and felt. I guess you never miss what you have never had. Now, as an adult I have met a handful of people who do experience the world as I do. Our kinship is very strong and we each recognise the responsibility we harbour.

It would have been wonderful for me to have had a contact with whom to share my experiences as a child. In his book "The Boy Who saw True," Cyril Scott explains his interpretation of the world, much like mine. I see life in vibrant colours, with a huge variety of sounds. Imagine if you can, trying to explain the differences to those who only see in black and white on their television screen, without sound, taste or touch, when your screen is in colour with sound, touch and taste too.

Many people have asked me what my childhood was like. As I try to recollect many memories, I realise that I was never childlike. I was always aware that I was a very old soul and

15

therefore had a knowing about being responsible for my actions. Until recently I had always had the feeling that I was responsible for others, in a huge way. In all honesty, I think there were times when I was too responsible and too sensible.

My earliest memories are of feeling and intuiting unbalanced energies, for me it was like listening to the screech of nails scratched on a blackboard. Now I realise that I received the information in order to send healing to the situation. Although I would know something was wrong, I would not know its whereabouts. This was very disconcerting, as I was never sure whether it was someone in my family who was affected or someone I did not know. Whether even it may have meant an international disaster was pending. It took me years to fine tune the interpretations of the energies.

Can you imagine being aware of energies, knowing there is a bad feeling and being really on edge for hours or even the whole day; without being sure what that awful sensation means, or could mean, for you directly, or those close to you?

It was only in 2002, as my spiritual journey began that through both the Tai Chi and when I had Reiki healer training, I had further understanding of energies. Now, when I feel an unease of energy, I consciously send healing and positive energy. Now I also have a deepened acceptance that all is as it should be.

The soul can leave the physical body of a person; the soul is still present and has a life of its own. The soul never dies. There are occasions when I still get agitated; although thankfully, these are now few and far between. The years of being in the dark, are at last over!!!

I did laugh like other children, though was never fully engrossed in the laughter. I was often distracted, picking up an imbalanced energy either from a person, people collectively or Mother Earth. I would then redress the balance and was never "switched off." I was extremely sensitive to people's moods too.

Although I had a knowing of energy fields, some were more difficult to interpret and being aware of the bigger picture was sometimes almost too much to bear. It's like information overload at times. . . . maybe for you it is similar to having the radio, the television and someone operating power tools nearby, whilst you trying to have a meaningful conversation!

I have known about disasters before they have happened and this has really made me feel incredibly uncomfortable. It was only when I was taught the Reiki that I realised I had been a healer all my life. I then had a means of understanding what I was doing when I was rebalancing energies and felt as though I had finally come home!

I was not aware at this time of past lives and to be honest, if the concept of past lives was mentioned I became really confused. Balancing and feeling energies was natural to me. If a place had negative energy, then I would re-dress the balance to ensure it was positive. I never realised that I was a healer.

It was just very natural to me. I remember being aware of energy lines in the Earth as a youngster, in fact when the children's father and I dated we would often spend our time balancing the local ley lines and feeling their whereabouts. It was normal to us, just as it is for an artist to paint I guess, or for a singer to sing, a dancer to dance.

Ley lines are energy lines in the Earth. Just as we have meridian lines in the body, so Gaia has energy lines to fuel/maintain her. Have you ever spoken to a farmer who has stated that no matter what fertilizer or crops they plant, there is always a place where they will not grow? It is usually in a corner or a field, though not always. You may have found the same in your own garden.

Maybe you feel a cold space in your house or a room that feels very uncomfortable? The energies are usually out of balance, it really is plain and simple. I am used as a conduit to hold and transfer energy to that particular place. I also transcend energy,

17

changing it from negative to positive. Often people ask if I can check out their homes or business premises. Frequently where houses have not been sold, despite having been on the market for some time, I am requested to visit and work my magic. . . . . in the nicest possible way of course. They often sell within days or even the same day.

I have many very vivid memories of evenings when I was unable to sleep. Lying awake for hours literally petrified when alien beings and ghouls would visit me. Night after night, this meant I lost many hours sleep as a youngster. I was terrified of the dark as a child, often sleeping with the light on all night.

I knew others did not see or hear what I saw; therefore there seemed very little point in explaining to my parents that I often lay terrified by presences of all kinds in the dark hours of the night and early hours of the morning.

My assumption was that they had come to frighten me, though I could never figure out why. Obviously now I do understand that they had come to receive healing.

As a homeopath I treat children in my practice who see and hear presences, see energies and are natural healers. It is a great privilege to work with them and to share experiences and help them in their understanding. To be honest, many parents without the insight I have, would probably have assumed I was crazy, marched me off to a psychiatrist or put me on drugs! Maybe they would have called the local priest in to help.

I feel now that it was for the best at the time that I kept these things to myself. I have been requested to help on many occasions when worried parents have said that their child has seen or heard something. I am always willing to help, maybe because I didn't have that support and understanding all those years ago. Many of these gifted, intuitive and in fact quite remarkable children are known as the Indigo/Crystal/Rainbow children. You probably know at least one, or maybe you were aware as a youngster.

The Goldfish That Jumped

As a young child I was brought up in the Roman Catholic faith. Most of my most vivid and earliest memories are of visiting our local church. The church itself is beautiful and usually we would attend mass weekly. I guess I must have been about three, maybe four years old and my earliest recollections are still amazingly vivid. I would often feel peaceful energies yet, when the sermons were read, I knew that they had been misinterpreted. Some of the priests' energy fields were dark and grey.

A spiritual teacher would truly have a bright, beautiful energy field. This is because when we have a connection to Source/God/ Angelic realms this is a light energy. It is vibrant and bright, loving, compassionate and enthusiastic, rather than heavy and sad, weighed down with guilt or doubt, fear or concern; dark and grey.

I have always seen auric fields, which are like a light or lights around the physical body. Years ago in the advertisement for "Ready Brek", the young boy who was featured had dull lights around him. Yet, after he had eaten the porridge the lights were glowing and beautiful.

The lights in an energy field are subtle, almost like a rainbow and they vibrate. Energy fields are individual to us, just as are our finger prints. Some are very similar, though no two are ever the same. They appear in different sizes, shapes and colours in varying shades and tones.

Some colours may be more prominent than others. They represent our life-force, our spiritual, mental and emotional awareness, our physical health and well-being and a wide range of other aspects of what we are collectively. I have learnt over the years that it is a huge responsibility seeing and interpreting an aura.

They will change according to our moods and emotions. They represent the well-being of that person, the Chi/ki/prana; which simply means life force energy in all aspects; mentally, physically, spiritually and emotionally. Essentially all these things collectively represent the soul. I have always seen the energy field first and foremost whenever I meet someone.

In my eyes, I see the persons' physical body secondly, after I have interpreted the aura. This is how I gauge their personality, mental, physical, spiritual and emotional well-being. By interpreting the colours, shapes and size of the aura, I know where I am safe and I have always known and understood what each colour, shade, etc., means. Learning to read people in this way allowed me to choose my friends carefully, wherever possible, keeping away from those with dark shaded auras.

Auras can be photographed using special cameras. Kirlian is probably the most well-known aura photography, it was invented in Russia. There are now many different types of energy cameras available. They are used to establish sell-by dates on fruit and vegetables as the larger the energy field of the fruit/veg the longer the shelf life will be.

The Light Inside the Darkness

"Some people walk in the rain. Others just get wet"

Roger Miller

I have always had a natural awareness of a knowing between interpreting a temporary drop in the auras size and shape and the difference in a permanent one. This is how I know if my patients are sick, very sick or terminally ill. It is a great responsibility; and, at times, one that has felt almost a curse.

Dark energy fields frightened me as a child and I have vivid recollections of those I particularly remember that were dark and damaged. Red energy fields represent anger at the deeper levels rather than just as a temporary state. The deeper and more powerful the red, so correspondingly the deeper the anger, becoming closer to rage.

I had a knowing that those with dark, brown/grey or black coloured auras were often pained with sadness, guilt, remorse, concern and fear; with little, if any connection to their soul. They would often be aggressive and abusive people, rarely smiling and generally unpleasant to be around. Of course there are various shades of grey/brown/black and each energy field is like a fingerprint: personal and individual. The darker the colour or colours the more dark the personality.

Most people feel energy fields to a point. We are each capable of thinking of those who have a bright personality rather than those with a dark cloud around them. Sometimes the dark vibration is caused by drugs – either conventional or recreational, addictive behaviours and or illness.

Whenever people have or are dabbling with black magic this is always represented here. In these circumstances the energy field perforates and becomes damaged. Though repairable, it takes time and a conscious effort on behalf of the person being healed.

As far back as I can remember I have seen things invisible to most people. I have always had a knowing of a deeper truth and religion NEVER sat comfortably with me. As a little girl, I remember sitting the church with some of the priests having grey, sometimes black, or near black, energy fields. It was more than enough to convince me that religious interpretation could be misleading.

The soulful, spiritual people, priests and religious leaders, have large, brightly coloured energy fields. They smile often and laugh, encouraging others to do the same. We do not have to attend religious ceremonies to be spiritual. How we live our life is reflective of our spirituality. Do we openly share, are we encouraging of others, how often do we welcome newcomers into our circle and do we live from the heart?

Misinterpreted teachings from the Bible were often fear-based. I knew Christ had not said the things they mentioned and felt as a child, that they were lies. At the times this used to anger me, as I knew Jesus' teachings were about joy and welcoming inspiration from the Soul. Why were the teachings in the church not mentioning these things? The teachings of Christ are very similar to those of Buddha, teachings about love, compassion and forgiveness.

Joy is encouraged and if you consider Buddhism, it is not a religion but a way of life. Many people become overwhelmed by religion; I was brought up Catholic and, as a child attended church on Sundays. Many people I met put on a smile for all the other church goers and once home returned to their soul-less, unhappy lifestyles. My dear mother knew someone who would attend church, and then go home to beat his wife!!!

My inner knowing meant that I knew that He had taught about heart-centred awareness, compassion, appreciation and joy. He taught about the gifts we have and the ability to share. It was all rather sad to me and although I used to enjoy going to church to a point I always left with a sense of confusion.

As a child I had been taught that adults told the truth and should be respected for this. Yet, I knew it was not the Truth. Usually children ask "WHY", funny because looking back I never recall asking mum, that question, I just accepted and held fast to my deeper knowing.

Many people over the years have questioned me on what religion I practice. "I was brought up as Roman Catholic, though I believe in the concepts of Buddhism", is usually my reply. I get many strange looks and comments when they receive my answer. Buddhism is not a religion; it is a way of life. It is a peaceful, honourable and heart-centred way of being.

In Gods eyes we are all the same. We all have freedom of choice and when I visit a place of worship I do it to pray for myself and others, in my own way. A way that feels right for me, a way in which I know that I am doing what is right for me and for others. I do not believe in living by obligation or by religious protocol. We each know what is right in our heart and soul. The only person we ever lie to is ourselves. No one person is better than another. It is our individual choice as to whether or not to aim to be a better person.

The Goldfish That Jumped

Living

"Don't exclude yourself....
from precious moments
warm encounters
beautiful attitudes
majestic discoveries
flowing intimacies
sensory development
for these are the jewels placed
in the crown of your destiny"

Walter Rinder

My advice to all; is to live life with your own knowing and integrity........... nothing more and absolutely nothing less.

If it feels right in your heart and soul it probably is. I have been amazed at some of the questions people have asked me over the years: "Will seeing you affect my religion?" "Do you use black magic?" "Are you a White Witch"? I use positive energies throughout my work. I have never used black magic though I do know of its power.

One lifetime many eons ago, through naivety I used it wrongly, thus I would never do it again. I don't really understand what a White Witch is, neither do I care. I work for the Highest Good at all times. "Will it affect my religion"? What a question!!! Was it true that Christ was a prophet and a healer?

Therefore, yes, it will hopefully make you a better person, because just maybe you might allow me to touch your soul. Sometimes I ask them "What do you think or feel?" Just in the hope that maybe, just maybe they will find their own truth, not someone else's impositions.

More recently I have been holding meditation classes and one member who was really blossoming and found connecting to his inner self a wonderful experience stopped attending the classes. I saw him a couple of weeks later and he said that he had asked his local priest what he thought of meditation. The priest had said it was devils work and this chap asked me about it. I was really surprised; if prayer is not meditation then what is it? Man-made laws and interpretations of the deeper truth get me off on my soap-box so I will end it here, before I go off on one!!!

The Early Years

*"What you love is a sign from your higher self
of what you are to do"*

Sanyana Roman

Many people have asked me about my psychic awareness and how it shaped me as a child. Most people think it is wonderful seeing and feeling what I experience. I honestly don't know what the masses intuit. My understanding comes from my own experiences, thus by listening and learning from others who are willing to tell me what they feel and sense, I learn from them and am learning how to help people to see, feel and respect their intuition.

Many ask me to teach them how to develop their psychic skills; I usually explain the responsibilities that go alongside with it and this usually helps them to realise that it is not as sweet and wonderful as is so easy to believe.

How I interpreted what I felt and my reactions to seeing spirits: this is a very complicated and difficult question to answer. I soon also learnt that other people could not see, hear and feel what I was consciously aware of. I can only assume that I learnt I was alone in my senses because other people did not respond to spirits and walked past or through them, totally ignoring them.

I was; and still am, to a large extent, unable to walk into places where the energies are seriously unbalanced and negative. Everyone else would walk without hesitation and fear. I, on the other hand would experience a terrible fear and recall being petrified on occasions. Feeling the dense energy and unpleasantness run throughout my body, I would shudder and cringe.

I have always had a knowing that we are not alone in The Universe. This was always just an acceptance in me. I loved watching Star Trek and reading Arthur C. Clarke. I recall watching any documentaries on extra-terrestrials and knowing they existed, even if there was a sense of disbelief from the presenter.

One thing which some people find peculiar is that although I had awareness that other people did not see, hear and feel what I saw, I honestly believed others saw energy fields. I was thirty six years old when I came to recognise that most do not. It was a real shock to me and I was rather gobsmacked. Why I had failed to be aware that others don't see them is not a question I can answer. For some reason I assumed they could. I really cannot explain this fact.

I have much to be grateful for to both my parents and grandparents. My mother is the eldest of six children so I learnt to interpret each of their energy fields and was surrounded by people with a wide range of interests and abilities.

My grandparents loved the great outdoors and encouraged all the family to do the same. As a child we used to venture to the local parks, Rivington and Pendle to name but a few day trips. Cousins, aunties and uncles and of course grandma and granddad would proudly take a hand in organizing these trips. For years our beloved granddad drove his three-wheeler car. (Yes, just like Rodney and Del Boy)!!

Granddad led the convoy of cars with the pride of a lion. We duly followed; usually one car per family, sharing each others' picnics and generally having a great time with my cousins. We played cricket, football the usual kids stuff. We NEVER went home before seven or eight pm and so, in this way, we made the most of each and every day.

Precious memories etched forever on my heart and soul. We visited many different places whilst allowed me to experience different energies of the environment. Some places were a pleasure to drive through and some more adverse.

Growing up with so many cousins around me was a means of me escaping into play. It *allowed me to* forget the weight of responsibility I was carrying. I was very lucky in that we would play on the local park and, as most of my cousins are males, I was great at cricket and not too bad at football. I even played in the rounder's team at our local school. I loved my cousins dearly and they were more like my brothers.

Most weekends, as families often do, we would all go out together, maybe to the local beach and mess about building sandcastles, swimming and splashing one another, catching crabs and trying to catch fish! Funny looking back I knew I was so very different to them, yet part of them at the same time.

Although I knew my cousin John was different, I never discussed anything of what I picked up with him. I had no language for my knowing, how or where would I start, I didn't think anyone would understand me or they may even think I was mad. Although I recognised my differences with them, I always knew I was part of them too. This is a contradiction I know; I am merely trying to explain myself as best as I can.

School however was very different. I remember very clearly my infant school teacher was very loving and had a huge white and gold energy field. She really did look like an angel to me and I always felt safe around her. She was a wonderful, soulful person. She had a knowing about her too. I often think of her now that I am an adult and give immeasurable thanks for that safe feeling she held in her presence. She was an inspiration to me and allowed me to flower as a child.

Teachers have a powerful influence over the children in their care. Often children spend more time with their teachers than they do with parents. It is wonderful when teachers understand energies and the power of their influence over the students.

Moving from the infant school to the junior school was a huge step for me. After three years, I left my beloved Mrs Robinson and moved to the junior school. It was much bigger and I had many more teachers. This meant more auras to interpret and decipher.

By this time I was beginning to know things about the future too which often scared me. Moving schools and having to accept various teachers' auras; some with extreme tiredness, stress, pain and sometimes representing physical illness was no easy task for a child that didn't feel she fitted in, didn't feel comfortable with the Catholic teachings and had nightmares on a regular basis.

The older I got the more isolated I became. The more I learnt to interpret energy fields, so the more I picked up on other people's emotional pain. I would always be aware if another pupil was having a hard time at home, if they were being bullied or feeling sad for whatever reason. I had no means of switching off that which I was aware of and constantly felt overwhelmed, heavy and actually very sad at the intensity of sadness around me. I was sad inside too; which is probably why I could associate with sadness so easily.

I often use the term "The Universe has it covered". When I began to attend the local high school you can imagine that I was overwhelmed by my intuition. I had no means of turning it off and often would have liked to adjust the volume lower.

One of the first teachers I met was my form teacher, Mr Rowe. I felt an immediate kinship and again had found a teacher that I felt safe to be around. As he was my form tutor this meant that I saw him first thing in the morning and last thing in the afternoon too. Throughout my five years at high school, he was my form teacher in all but one of the years. He was also my English Language and English Literature teacher.

To this day, I still hold a huge amount of gratitude for such a wonderful man. Those five years, from aged 11 to 16 are so powerful. We develop from child to a young adult. The physical changes alone are enough to have to cope with but my intuition was, by now, on overdrive. Again getting used to the wide varieties of auras and personalities of the teachers was overwhelming.

I remember that I was quite good at history but didn't feel that I could manage to do this subject because the teacher had an intense dislike of me, and, in all fairness, it was mutual. Now I understand that she was there to prevent me from studying history as it would have probably have opened "a can of worms" with regard to past life déjà vu. This is explained in later chapters.

My music teacher was a very nice lady indeed. She always had a huge smile for everyone too. It was both amazing and painful to watch her energy field change, and deteriorate, when she went through a divorce. By this point I was getting used to interpreting and accepting auras.

Some stand out more than others. We had a clarinet teacher visit the school occasionally to deliver clarinet lessons. His energy was serene and peaceful. He was a joy to be around. Two of the art teachers fell in love and eventually married; watching their energy fields when they were together was awesome. . . . that being "in love" feeling meant that their auras were huge!

Mr Rowe was my hero and unfortunately one day, as I caught a glimpse of him I knew something was very, very wrong. The year head came in to explain that he had witnessed a road traffic accident earlier that morning, and alternative arrangements were being made for our teachings that day. I soon learnt how to interpret shock in the energy system. He was allowed home for the day and, when he returned his energy had returned to normal.

School policies are ever changing, when I was younger a decision was made that we would be the first students ever, to take our 'O' level English language a year early. The reason was that it would be one less for the following year and would thus be less stressful for us.

As with many exams now there was a lot of coursework involved, making up 50% of the total mark. English language meant that much was accredited to our creative writing. I recall one essay title that just seemed to consume me whilst I wrote the story. We were usually given a week or two before they were sent off for examination. This story was open, there was no title, just a sentence to lead us in to the story which was "As I approached the door" or something very similar.

The story came to me very quickly and I was both excited, yet disturbed at the same time. The images I created relating from this story had lots of energy and seemed very real. The story was in my dreams too, the characters appearing real. At other times, quite often when I was in different lessons, other than English, I would make notes as to what would happen next. It was particularly different to anything I have ever experienced.

The story began explaining to the reader, that the main character in the book was a lady in her mid-twenties, happily married to her soul partner. Her husband and her father got on very well, and her husband was treated as though he was a son to beloved father.

Unfortunately, her father had been widowed after many years in a very happy marriage. Following this he had retired from work, having accumulated a great deal of wealth. He lived alone in a large property, some way away.

They were a very close, loving family. Her father had had his own business, though always managed to balance work and family commitments. He always loved time spent with his family. He and her dear mother, when she was alive, were very close and affectionate, they were great friends too. The main character had suggested that her beloved father move nearer to her and her husband.

She was aware that he might become lonely following the widowhood. The drive was approximately two and a half hours, so, as she and her husband worked full time, it wasn't so easy to travel on a daily basis, although they did see each other at least once weekly.

She telephoned him either daily or every other day and they had a wonderful relationship. Her father had always been a most grounded man. He was also a philanthropist and very balanced gentleman. The story was written through the eyes of the daughter.

More recently he had started to act in an odd manner when they had visited and he seemed distant and withdrawn. When she spoke to him on the phone, he had seemed almost agitated, as though something had worried him greatly. Being a grounded, balanced man, he usually coped with ALL things; even her mother's death.

She was becoming increasingly disturbed that her father seemed more and more distant. This became much more concerning when he begun to ask her lots of questions relating to the occult. This subject had never interested him before and she knew very little about it. The feelings of worry for his welfare and mental health were growing daily.

Every week they spoke regularly on the phone at least four times, usually at the weekend she and her husband looked forward to going to visit him. One particular day he failed to answer the telephone. They had agreed when they would be speaking again so this seemed unusual. Her concern was ever increasing, especially when, later that day he still failed to answer the telephone.

Eventually they managed to chat and he mentioned that he had met a woman who was able to answer many of his questions relating to the occult. Although he said he was fine, his voice and mannerisms seemed different. Time went on and she telephoned again several days later. There was no reply.

The powerfulness of the winter season was very much at its peak. It was a dark, bitterly cold and icy month. Rarely had there been any sunshine and, day after day, the news was focused on weather warnings, traffic jams and advice about keeping warm and being considerate of the elderly and infirm. As her father lived alone, she was becoming more and more alarmed that she could not contact him. In desperation, despite the weather and the icy roads, she and her husband travelled the distance across country to ensure he was well.

Upon their eventual arrival they noticed the huge wooden door was slightly ajar. As they entered the house, it was deathly quiet and there was no sign of life at all. Her heart was racing and her eyes became filled with tears. Her intuition had been right. As they moved through into the lounge, they noticed that strewn all over the huge coffee table were books on the occult.

As she looked across at her husband, her stomach churned, concern was etched on his face too. They checked around the whole of the house, each little cupboard, under the stairs, nothing was left to chance. If he was there they had to find him. Panic filled the air and both she and her husband were frightened for his welfare. They moved into the frozen, frosty garden. Despite the beautiful sight of the icicles and frosted plants and shrubs, nothing could distract them from their mission; to locate her father. However, it was to prove fruitless, there were no signs of him. They desperately checked the garage. That too was empty.

The house was freezing, the central heating had not been switched on and the open fires had obviously not been lit for more than two days. They had searched throughout the whole house. Nothing. His bed was made and nothing was out of place. After tidying the books and lighting the open fires, they were drawn to check the answering machine. There was a message from a woman saying that she would like to meet him, this had been on the machine for days.

Looking through the fridge the milk was beginning to sour, several items were out of date and there was a peculiar smell – surely something was very, very wrong. She decided to telephone the local police and reported her beloved father as a missing person. He had lived here for many years and was a well-respected member of the community. She was desperate to know what had happened. She kept expecting her father to walk through the door and was looking forward to seeing his lovely, warm, welcoming face again. Yet, inside she knew something was indeed very wrong.

Night-time came and still nothing. Both she and her husband were deeply upset and worried. They tossed and turned most of the night. In the early hours of the morning, the restlessness got the better of them and they both went downstairs. They had a cup of tea and decided on a plan that at first light, they would go out and look for her father. At dawn they dressed in multiple layers of their warmest clothes and their thickest coats. It was bitterly cold and ice hung from the gutters and frost to the trees.

As they left the house, not really knowing where and how far they were to venture, they wandered about the local area. She slipped several times on the ice and found tears in her eyes as she thought of all the precious times she had spent with her father. What had become of him? How would she ever cope without him in her life? Losing her mother was painful enough and she really didn't feel that she could cope without her precious father.

They had walked for several hours and despite being cold, struggled against the winter weather and its harshness. She came across a group of people in a local park. They were gathered around a pond. She assumed that they had been ice-skating on the frozen water.

Yet when she approached her sense of knowing that something was wrong grew ever stronger and she began to feel nauseous. She gripped her husbands' hand tightly as they drew nearer. The crowd were gathered and some were sighing and making strange gasping sounds. She wondered if perhaps someone had fallen into the water. Then, as they got even closer it became obvious that there was a body floating, face down in the water. It was the body of a man, broad shoulders and smartly dressed.

The Goldfish That Jumped

She thought she recognised the coat. Then she realized it was her dear father, lying face down in that water. She was so horrified and overtaken by shock and grief she screamed and screamed. Her husband pulled her closer and hugged her with all his might. Her worst fears were confirmed, she had known in her soul that he was dead, now she was here looking out at her dead father.

The police had already been called and eventually the site was cordoned off. The post-mortem revealed that he had been in the water for almost three days. They could never say how it had happened, it remained a mystery. He had been a fit, healthy and sensible man. Therefore why would he be out walking in freezing weather conditions?

There was no sign of him having been pushed or having fallen in the water. His daughter and her husband never found the answers they were looking for and the whole situation was just left open-ended, rather like an open wound.

The morning I handed in that particular essay I will remember for the rest of my life. It had taken over my life in the last fortnight and I was really glad to hand it in and breathed a sigh of relief that life could go on as normal. I soon came to realize how wrong I was.

I had literally just given the essay to Mr Rowe when the head teacher came into the classroom explaining that another teacher had died. He had been missing for several days and his body had been found in frozen water. The other circumstances were listed in the press later that week and he had died following a period of odd behaviour.

I don't remember what happened after I received the news. I broke down in floods of tears with shock and trauma of what I had just heard. Mr Rowe took me to one side and offered me support and great understanding. I explained to him the details of the dead man in my story and he gently assured me that, as it was wintertime anyone could make this assumption in an essay.

In a very garbled manner, explained that this kind of prophecy work was second-nature to me and that I saw things and heard things too. I explained that this particular piece of work had taken over my life and I was aware of slightest details of what I would include in the story both day and night.

He listened and then confided that he too saw ghosts and heard things. Although surprised I was very pleased that he didn't think I was going crazy and I will always be grateful for the support he gave me that particular day. Years later we bumped into each other on Preston railway station quite by chance. He and I discussed our gifts openly and I had an opportunity to thank him.

I finished high school in 1983, achieved the qualifications as expected and moved on to Runshaw Tertiary College to study A levels. The change was huge, I met so many new people and the whole ambience of the place was incredibly different.

I was studying Sociology, Biology and Home Economics in the hope that I would later take up a career as a dietician or in nursing. Being at college was entirely different to the routine of school. The discipline now was about us as students taking personal responsibility.

I have never had a problem with self-discipline and actually enjoyed the balance and sense of freedom this gave me. Having chosen to study my favourite subjects was very appealing to me and meant I felt settled. I was being recognised as an adult now and this was the next step forward in my life at that time.

Sociology was my favourite subject and I took to it like a duck takes to water. I loved it and at the end of the first year had achieved a Grade A in my mock exams. Thus was expected to gain Grade A in the A level exam the following year.

Home Economics was interesting though challenging on occasions. I did love the subject though and got on extremely well with my fellow students. Biology was tough at times and I really had to work hard at my studies. There was very little comparison between biology as a subject that we had studied at school and that studying at college.

I still recall clearly dissecting a rat and studying its anatomy and physiology. Now, with much more awareness of all living things and their souls, I send a big apology to all ratty friends! My closest friend Jeannette really struggled with the ethics of this particular part of the syllabus. In order to calm her I would always say "Just imagine it's a carrot." Over 25 years later, whenever we meet we still laugh at the bloody carrot!!!!

As I said I have never had a problem with self-discipline. It amazed me to see other students deliberately choosing to miss lessons or a whole day. I guess looking back I was a real "goodie two shoes," in all respects.

There was one lesson in biology though that I could not attend. The worm dissection. Nothing could have made me attend that lesson!!! It was the only time I bunked off college, wandering through the local park in a state of fear at the mere thought of others handling and touching them.

From a very early age I have had a real phobia of worms, if I ever saw one crawling near me I would be consumed with terror. I used to think they would kill me. Whereas other children would dig and play with worms, I never could. I was unable to look at them, never mind even considering the thought of touching them. YUK.

One particular childhood memory stands out very clearly. I awoke one morning very early to the sound of the twin tub washing machine, on the spin cycle in the kitchen. Mum greeted me and I went into the bathroom for the usual early morning pee. We lived in a bungalow which, being on a corner plot, had gardens surrounding all sides. It was beautiful and the front garden was full of English roses which were mums pride and joy.

My youngest brother, Martin, then aged about three years old, loved the great outdoors and thoroughly enjoyed the freedom of the garden. I was about ten years old and Martin had been up for over an hour, playing in the garden and digging up worms. I finished in the bathroom and duly washed my hands. I then proceeded into the kitchen to get my breakfast.

At the same time Martin was coming into the kitchen with a bucket full of wriggling worms!!! I was filled with absolute terror. I screamed and screamed uncontrollably, crying and shaking, I rushed into the bathroom, begging mum not to let him near me I locked myself in crying, screaming and in a state of absolute panic. I kept screaming, "They'll kill me mum, please don't let them near me."

Sensible thought and logic had completely left me. As the house was a bungalow, the overflow pipe was on the ground floor, so, consumed by terror, I was convinced that Martin would find my reaction so amusing that in order to maintain and increase the level of my fear, he would place the worms in the overflow and they would then somehow seek me out and harm me.

I had visions of being covered in worms which would very quickly kill me. Mum tried to reassure me that he had gone outside and taken the worms with him, that I was safe to unlock the door and come out. I honestly do not recall how long I spent in the bathroom that morning; crying, sobbing and shaking uncontrollably.

I made enough noise to awaken the whole household, not to mention the neighbours who must have thought I was being tortured. Little did I realise at that time how true this insight was to become.

Even as I type this now I feel a deep sickness in my throat. . . . . . get the bucket!!! It was only years later, aged 40 that I was given the understanding of why this was my biggest fear at the time.

Looking back I enjoyed my college years. I had been in the church and school choir and as such had met students from different parishes. Early in 1984 my friend Jackie introduced me to her group of friends, one member clearly stood out. Tall, gorgeous and handsome, he stood out like a beacon in the group. No surprise that his birthday is Valentine's Day!

Little did I know then, that within three years we would be married and would have started to bring up our own family. I guess I loved him the first time I met him. We instantly "clicked" and laughed often, spending time in the park and surrounding area. Wherever we were, we were always happy to be. He accepted me totally for who I was and I gained a lot of comfort and confidence from his understanding. He was also aware of energies and we often balanced ley line energies, happy to spend most of our time in the great outdoors. We were very much in love and spent as much time as possible together.

The A level courses were for two years; in the summer term of 1984 I contracted glandular fever. I had certainly done a lot of kissing!!! It is known as "The Kissing Disease," for a reason. This was a particularly severe case of the illness and I spent the following two weeks in bed; sleeping. I was ill all through the summer and still had not recovered by the time of the September term. It threatened to thwart my studies completely.

Two weeks after the September term started, I returned to college. I was physically exhausted and drained, struggling to walk between lectures and finding it even harder to concentrate. Sociology had been my favourite subject and now I had entered my second year I could hardly recall what I had learnt in the previous year.

I remember asking repeated questions about main topics that I had previously known thoroughly. I had been a star pupil, now I knew my tutor felt that I was a nuisance. It was so very frustrating, yet, when I look back, I was too exhausted even to get frustrated! I continued to struggle on for months and although I passed my exams failed to gain the expected grades. Since this time I had been advised that following such an acute attack of glandular fever, students are advised to take a year off from their studies.

Timothy and I continued our relationship even though I was so ill. He was always patient and understanding towards me. His mother was also aware of energies and she had introduced me to dowsing. We set up The Lancashire Society of Dowsers and I met lots of interesting people. We offered a dowsing for health service: which I found I was especially capable of doing. I would often give detailed reports on illnesses and would send healing.

Ironic now when I look back because all the information was there for me to understand and accept that I was a healer. If I had had more insight then I would have maybe followed it through and began my career as a healer earlier. Who knows. . . . . again, The Universe had other ideas. The society ran for a few months and then folded.

Timothy and I became engaged in Christmas 1985 and married the following spring. Our daughter would arrive later that year. I had always wanted four children and also wanted to have my family close together to get that part of my life out of the way, knowing I would be doing other things at a later date. . . . . how true!!!

Just before we married in 1986, my parents were looking for another home. I recall clearly mum asking me to view several properties with her. One in particular stands out. It was a lovely sunny, spring morning and as we approached the front door, mum knocked gently explaining I was her daughter and she wanted a second opinion.

The house was a lovely 1950's semi-detached. We were welcomed into the hall way and then through into the lounge and dining room, then the kitchen. As we approached the kitchen I began to shake violently and felt a very cold chill race around my body. I shivered violently and rushed out of the house as quickly as possible. Mum dashed out after me, probably wondering what on earth was wrong! I explained that the house seemed lovely but that I couldn't settle and would never be able to visit, though if she wanted to buy the house that would be okay with me. I didn't really understand what I had felt, merely that I knew I had to leave urgently and was actually scared too.

She decided not to purchase the house and opted for one literally around the corner. Overtime, someone else bought the property and they moved in, eventually extending the kitchen. The family became good friends of my parents. One day it was mentioned that when they had dug the foundations for the new extension they had recovered the remains of a baby. Mum's face was a picture when she relayed the story to me!

Timothy and I were childhood sweethearts and as such were just finding our feet in life. He was training as a masseur and also as a painter and decorator. I was a domestic goddess and soon to be mother. Despite always wanting to have a career in healthcare, I had other priorities with a new born daughter expected soon and I felt I should be a full-time mother.

I had always known that I would have four children: a daughter and three sons. I didn't want a big age gap between the children and the boys arrived one after the other. So, as I had predicted, I had my children in four and a half years. Bringing up four young children was both amazing and exhausting too.

During this time my energies were obviously concentrated on my family. Tim was very aware of my gift and had intuitive gifts of his own. He was very understanding, especially as I often became very upset and felt uncomfortable if a national or international disaster was about to happen.

I recall knowing something really bad would happen on the day of the Lockerbie disaster and just paced the street for about an hour. I knew to the minute when it happened, weird as it may seem, I was then calm. We would just watch the news and wait for confirmation.

Over those years there were many instances which would surprise, and occasionally frighten me relating to my intuition. Many pale into insignificance as they were so frequent. However, one particular instance will always stand out for against many others. From an early age I was afraid of the dark and always preferred to sleep with the light on. Often my room would be filled with spirits and alien beings whom had come to receive healing.

However, at this time I was unaware of my healing abilities, thus they just frightened me. So, even when I married Tim, I was still very scared of the dark and he knew he would always be the one to have to turn the light off before getting into bed at night. If I ever needed to get up through the night he would have to be the one to turn the light on for me too. Eventually we got bedside lamps though it was always a standing joke and the whole family knew of my fear relating to the dark.

One particularly cold, wet and windy December evening, he and his brother were celebrating their Christmas works do. I was in the early stages of pregnancy with our eldest son and was exhausted. Emily was a toddler so every day was a busy one. I have never been a night-owl anyways and have always needed plenty of sleep. I knew there was no point waiting up for him as it would be at least midnight before they returned. Soon after he left the house, I checked on our daughter, locked the house and went upstairs to bed.

As usual I was soon fast asleep. It was the early hours of the morning, when I awoke suddenly with a knowing that he had been killed. Over many years I had learnt not to ignore my insights, I was horrified at the thought of losing him. I knew it had been a car accident and that it had been instant. I lay there wondering what to do. How would I cope without my husband, my best friend? How would I manage with Emily and a youngster on the way? I couldn't phone anyone at this early hour so; I would just have to wait for news.

It was awful and each second seemed like an hour. I tried to think logically and decided I could do nothing. Therefore the most sensible thing to do was sleep as I had to get up the following day and would have to sort out everything then. I tried which was obviously fruitless, and I was, by this time really beginning to realise the implications of my pending fate. Timothy was too young to die and I was mortified at the thought. So, without lighting, I walked downstairs and waited.

I paced the lounge and the dining room, the emotions welling up second by second. No sounds in the street outside, no phone call either. I reasoned this was stupid and decided to return to bed. Try as I might, I couldn't sleep, the feelings were getting ever stronger. I was really concerned for the whole situation now and was actually beginning to panic. My heart raced as I thought about what energies I was passing to my unborn baby.

Being a widow at twenty years old certainly did not appeal to me. I paced the rooms again, in the dark. My mind raced and I had begun to shake violently and uncontrollably. The shock was consuming my being. I heard a sound outside and assumed it to be the police. As I moved from one room to the other, there was the sound of the key in the door.

Then Tim and his brother walked in the house. "You look like you have seen a ghost, are you alright? Why are you shaking? What are you doing in the dark?" I began to cry tears of relief and clung to him for dear life. "Have you almost been killed?" "Yes," they replied. "Less than ten minutes ago?" I questioned, "Yes," they replied in unison. "We were just passing the town hall and someone went through on a red light, incredibly fast and missed us by a whisker."

I shall never forget their faces as they then realised why I was shaking and looked like I had seen a ghost. My brother in law never questioned my abilities following that night. If I ever gave a warning it was always noted and followed.

The Tiananmen Square disaster happened on my 22nd birthday. We were on holiday at the time and staying in accommodation without a TV or radio. Neither of us was interested in newspapers although this particular day I was much more aggravated than normal. It was only later that day when we overheard the news in a public place that we understood the gravity of what had happened.

The Goldfish That Jumped

I was deeply saddened and that feeling still feels as powerful now as it did back then. That was a feeling that stayed with me for days and left me feeling raw and pained at man's inhumanity to man.

The awareness with my children was, and still is amazing. I knew the moment I conceived my eldest son. I also knew that he was ready to be delivered as my waters had broken though were just a trickle. I was admitted to the labour ward and explained to the doctor that he was ready to come and my body wasn't responding. He was incredibly arrogant and although I should have been checked for leaking amniotic fluid that morning, before being discharged, I was allowed to return home.

Needless to say, although I didn't know I was a healer then, I obviously was and must have sent healing to my unborn son. He was born a week later than the due date and the midwives were amazed that he was fit and well as the amniotic fluid was infected and he was covered in spots. The power of any mother's intuition should never be underestimated.

My second son arrived following a difficult and very long labour. I was exhausted and had lost a lot of blood. He was a very long baby and no matter how much he ate, always remained very skinny. When I attended the baby clinics with him I would be embarrassed, as his ribs were always clearly visible.

No matter how much he ate, he would always remain thin. He was such a beautiful child with lovely curly hair. However, when he screamed, he really screamed, and often there was no reason at all. I soon became aware that one particular reason for the screaming was related to his blood sugar.

The children were all fed on demand and I never left them until mealtimes. If they were hungry, they ate when they wanted food, not just at set times. As his blood sugar dropped the screaming would commence. We were all upset by this behaviour.

I was a kind, caring and receptive mother, and, as such found this very distressing. It was embarrassing too, as often we would

45

be out somewhere and randomly this screaming would begin. The times people stared at us thinking we were bad parents was incredibly frequent! He walked at nine months and hid food all over the house.

When he was a toddler, I would find food under his bed, in his pockets, anywhere and everywhere. He always looked too skinny and malnourished. Even now, almost twenty one years of age, he has food with him wherever he goes. He is still skinny and his ribs are still visible too. The reason for this behaviour was eventually to be explained in a reading some twelve years later.

I knew I would have four young children. Matthews' birth had been very traumatic and he was such a difficult baby and toddler that I was not really considering having any more children at all. This created a deep sadness in my soul, yet I knew everything would turn out for the best.

My daughter was four, eldest son two and Matthew was a toddler. We had our hands full and I wondered how we would ever manage another child anyway. Day to day washing, cleaning, cooking and especially bath times were very demanding. The Universe always has a bigger plan.

Tim and I were discussing sterilisation, as I really felt that there would be no further additions to our family. At the time, mid October 1990, I was feeling really very tired, quite sickly and had missed three monthly menses. I decided to go to the doctors for a check up. Obviously the doctors' first thoughts were that I was pregnant. I stated very clearly, that I could only just cope with the three I had, never mind anymore, so therefore I could not possibly be pregnant. Clearly, the doctors' suggestion was ridiculous!

The joke was to be on me! He suggested he examine my tummy and of course felt the size of the uterus. "You're about 12-14 weeks pregnant, so we will have to book you in to ante-natal clinic as soon as possible." I was really shocked and began to cry. I couldn't believe it and even suggested to the doctor that he was lying to me!!!

Looking back we still laugh at the situation. I must have known I was pregnant and yet denied it to myself. I wandered around the local park for quite some time. How was I going to cope? How would my husband take the news? He had always said, every bath time; which you can imagine were busy and challenging, that if I ever became pregnant again, he would leave. Here I was thinking thoughts of how on earth I would manage with four little ones.

I was very scared and as most pregnant women know, would have been emotional anyway, due to the influence of the pregnancy hormones. What a dilemma. I wondered how I would tell him, my family and close friends.

After several hours of wandering aimlessly, I made my way home. He had been very concerned for my welfare and was pleased to see me. "Well, what did the doctor say then?" "I'm pregnant. . . again." I blurted and began to cry. He was delighted and immediately went to tell the neighbours!!!

I was still shocked and trying to get my head round the idea of how I would manage with four small children under the age of five. The baby was due the following spring sometime, although a scan would give us a more accurate date. I was very fearful of labour again and knew I couldn't possibly cope with the problems I had had with Matthew.

As time went on I gradually accepted things and actually had a great pregnancy too. He was overdue and so I was admitted to hospital to be induced. I had prayed for help and for an easy labour. As it turned out, Philip arrived within two hours and ten minutes of my being induced. It was quick and easy and virtually pain free by comparison to Matthews' labour. I did not have post-partum haemorrhage and felt very well following delivery too.

The children were wonderful and this new born baby so easy it was a blessing. Whenever he fell asleep during the day, he would be wakened up by his siblings, thus he slept through the night at a very early age. He was an easy baby and very manageable child too. In fact, we managed the daily family domesticities very well indeed. If only I knew then, what I know now, I could have trusted in The Universe, rather than worrying for no good reason.

Finances were limited and Tim was in and out of work. My friend worked in the Civil service at the time and mentioned that there was a huge advertising campaign for new recruitment. It was a difficult decision to make to apply for full-time employment.

My youngest son was 17 months old and ideally I would have loved to have stayed at home until he had gone to school. Practically however, I felt I would have to apply and hoped that I was successful. With mouths to feed and bills to pay, I felt that I had no other choice.

I started work as an Administration Officer in the Civil service in 1992. I loved it for many years. Unfortunately, within a year and a half of me commencing work, the marriage was failing fast. It was an incredibly sad time and we were both so young. Hindsight is a wonderful thing and, who knows, maybe we married too young, maybe there were too many problems, maybe lack of communication.

I believe there were many reasons for the breakdown and that was a very difficult decision to make, knowing that I would be mainly responsible for four young children. The divorce was finalized in 1995.

I was in my late twenties, still a baby myself by all accounts and terrified of my future and how I would manage. I lived in fear of what would become of us and I can honestly say now that I don't know how I kept the family together. At that time, it was the most difficult thing in my life to deal with.

Following the divorce, the children and I moved house in order that I was nearer my parents as I needed their support and help. Managing four children, working full-time, managing a home and doing household maintenance and improvements were real challenges and it was a huge juggling act. I lived a life of worry, constant stress and was often run down. Support from my parents was very gratefully received and appreciated.

I was very happy with my family though I wanted to find that "Mr Right." I felt he was out there somewhere and, again hindsight would have been a wonderful awareness to have at the time. I thought I would find my soul-mate and he would fix me, in exchange for me fixing him. It took me many years and several relationships to realise that the only person who could fix me was ME.

Whilst in the Civil Service I kept my intuitive abilities mostly private. Only my closest friends knew of my gift. One particular occasion stands out to me for a variety of reasons: the main one being religious rules and protocol. I worked on a small team and we each relied on one another intensely. The manager was a delight to work for and the team very close.

One of the girls was a Jehovah's Witness and I had been pre-warned that she would try to convert me. In all fairness, she never did try, probably because she sensed from me that I certainly wouldn't be interested in the slightest. We became friends and over the weeks she explained that she had cared for her mother-in-law before her prolonged death. I could see her late relative stood behind her and asked if she'd ever felt her around. "Oh no" was her very swift reply, "We're not allowed to believe any of that nonsense."

I tried again a few days later, explaining that they had obviously been very close and it might be a suggestion, to maybe, be a little open minded. The spirit of her dead mother-in-law desperately wanted to communicate her thanks, and would regularly stand beside her whilst she worked. I quickly learnt to say nothing more to her and apologised to the spirit, explaining that I had tried and was unable to do anymore.

My time in the Civil service was coming to a close although, at the time I had no idea how soon it would be. After almost ten years of the politics and various restructures, I recognised that it had all caused a real unrest in my soul. I decided to place a request for an internal transfer to the Inland Revenue for Working Families Tax Credits, as it was then. It was successful and extremely speedy too.

However, the job I had done previously was very complicated and offered me a challenge. The new job however, was all automated and computer based. It bored me to tears and although I loved the team I worked with I was close to despair. Day after day was just the same old monotony and became a real chore. However, whilst on that particular team, I was introduced to a man who was very aware of his past lives and the Holy Grail which is said to be the bloodline of Christ.

We became great friends and we each experienced more déjà vu just by being together. Finally I had met someone who was aware. Unfortunately, his private life was very fraught at the time and our friendship dwindled over time. I still appreciate everything I learnt and experienced from him.

Then one day, whilst I sat looking out of the window at a single tree, thinking of my beloved Derwentwater, my guides very loudly and clearly stated "You will do psychic readings." My very swift and assertive reply was "No, I won't, I have four children to support and a mortgage." The voice repeated itself again and my reply remained the same. I actually didn't think much of it at the time and was quite unwilling to change or even to consider their request. So, again, instead of making life easy for myself and listening and being open-minded, I chose to do it my way, and, in turn The Universe took control.

Realisation of Truth

"Allow life to be the theatre of god,
in which what seems appropriate and necessary
in your case will be accomplished spontaneously.
You must trust the process of your own life. "

Heart-Master Da Love-Ananda

My Soul's journey started in 2002. My relationship had broken down on New Year's Eve 2001 – I certainly didn't appreciate the timing. He left, and I spent New Year's Day alone – it was ultimately the beginning of my year and the beginning of my Soul's journey. I was being forced to go within myself as I knew that I could NO longer carry on doing what I had always done.

"If we always do what we always did, we always get what we always got". It was obvious now that my behaviour was certainly not serving me anymore and that I had to change.

Looking within was to be very painful, and the realisation that I had caused all of what had happened even more so. However, at that time I had no choice. It was time to change, sink or swim. My children were to prove to be my anchor in a huge storm which raged between anger, at myself, rage, at myself and guilt, at all the things I had done wrong.

Fear of change was also mixed into the storm somewhere too. So, all in all, I was embracing the worst energies we can ever hold, fear, doubt, guilt and worry for my future and that of my children. Not an easy combination and certainly a journey through troubled waters. It was to be a journey of my lifetime: My Inner Journey.

Taking a closer look at me, especially the negative aspects; I was always great at focusing on them. It was a journey which eventually led me to the present day and, of course is on-going.

There is a saying:

"Religion is for those who fear Hell;
Spirituality is for those who have been to Hell".

After divorcing my husband in 1995 I'd had a handful of short-term relationships; each ending on MY TERMS. I had too high expectations & felt that EACH relationship would magically restore my wholeness. I expected someone else to put me back together. However, I was foolish enough to believe that was possible.

So, after my divorce, I was frightened and broken; instead of giving time and energy to myself, to heal, I gave it away in my relationships in the hope that this would allow me to become whole. I bumbled from one short-term relationship to another. In spirituality there is a saying that to become whole-hearted we must first be broken hearted. I had been heading down that road very, very fast indeed.

For the first time ever I was about to apply the handbrake! I knew I had to look after ME, a completely new concept. We are creatures of habit and often struggle with change. I was forced to change because my behaviour was certainly too destructive to my well-being and that of my children. Enough was most definitely enough!

So, that New Year's Day 2002, my inner Hell commenced. I was emotionally worn-out, tired to my core and knew things had to change. *I had to change.* I remember being asked: as you are so psychic, why were you unaware of the outcome? I am as vulnerable as the rest of the population, in all aspects, especially in relationships.

I certainly felt they would most likely end, despite this I continued to put all my efforts in. I was so desperate to find the perfect partner. They do not exist; now I realize that on a spiritual level with a much deeper understanding.

A soul mate is very different to a soul companion. We can honour our selves by realizing that our own imperfections will be reflected very painfully back to us in a soul mate. A soul companion will accept us for *all* that we are and will encourage us to grow when we are challenged. Their inspiration and support allows us to appreciate our weaknesses as part of who we are. They encourage us to enhance our strengths and accept ourselves in the process.

In my mind I held the thought that by loving and healing my partner's pain, I, in turn would be healed by them. Like attracts like; I was broken and kept attracting in broken people. When we are broken we can heal no-one, but ourselves. Now I see the foolishness of this – hindsight is truly a wonderful gift!

The phrase "women who love too much" springs to mind: I needed to be healed of all my emotional pain and trauma and had become co-dependent on a most unreliable partner. I had based that relationship on NEED, not love in the true sense.

The only person to blame was ME. I never ONCE considered how much love I gave away; neither had I ever considered how I could love and nurture MYSELF; most important of all, I had not considered how much I had denied myself the feeling of being loved. I did not accept myself for all that I was at that time, so how could someone else be expected to? I failed to comprehend at this time that I did not accept myself.

So I attracted partners who did not accept or understand themselves. Counsellors call this "mirroring". My mirror reflected back all its cracks and blemishes. Looking back it has been quite a colourful journey of restoration needing much tender, loving care. This latest disaster had been the straw that finally broke the camel's back.

I cried like a baby, felt suicidal and I finally began to understand that the only person to answer my needs on the road to wholeness was ME. For the first time ever I had to go WITHIN. I HAD TO HEAL MYSELF. I held all the answers; I just needed to look inside to find them. I made a vow then that I would *not get* involved again in a relationship until I was healing, or healed.

How do we ever know when we are healed?

How do we know when we are complete, whole and *able to function without carrying all the emotional baggage that distracts us from who we really are?*

Ideally we should live without fear, honour our true identity, potential, our creativity, and accept our vulnerabilities as part of our wholesomeness.

Our greatest gift to ourselves is TO BE. Our greatest gift to others is also TO BE.

"Our deepest fear is not that we are inadequate. Our deepest fear is that we are powerful beyond measure. It is our Light – not our darkness that most frightens us. Your playing small does not serve the world, there's nothing enlightened about shrinking so that people won't feel insecure around you. We were all meant to shine as children. It's not just in some of us, it's in everyone, and, as we let our own light shine we unconsciously give others permission to do the same. As we are liberated from our own fear, our presence automatically liberates others".

Marianne Williamson

Rebirth

"What would it be like if you lived each day, each breath,
as a work of art in progress?
Imagine that you are a masterpiece unfolding,
every second of every day a work of art
taking form with every breath."

Thomas Crum

This book "My Inner Journey" is of how I stumbled into spirituality: the journey of the Soul. Of how I came to believe and UNDERSTAND past lives and how they can - and do, influence us. It is also about how I came to understand the spiritual laws: the workings of the Universe, karma: the way in which we create our own destiny and the situations around us, at any given time. This is MY TRUTH – it does not have to be yours. My hope is that by reading and allowing this book to touch your soul, then, maybe, it will open you to your Higher Self; on some level at least.

By living from the soul the world becomes a better place. We each can master our own destiny using the Power of Creation, God given to each and every one of us. Trust in that knowing, find your path and your life's journey will be filled with miracles along its way. I come merely as a messenger to relight your inner flame bringing a deeper knowing; to reawaken your sleeping soul, to rekindle your spiritual flame.

I hope this book brings an understanding of healing and of how we can each touch one another: on so many profound levels. The journey begins and ends with us – I hope this book is a welcome hand which holds yours firmly, tightly and lovingly.

Onwards and upwards, and, as my very dear friend Jack says, "Keep smiling."

It is often the dark times in our lives that give us our most valuable learning. The dark nights of the Soul can become our most powerful times of learning about our inner strength. Whilst in this space we learn about our wholeness, the good, the bad and the indifferent too. We learn our strengths and weaknesses, our talents and our potential. We simply learn TO BE. My book is about how I learnt to find my power. This quote is my favourite, I love it and relate to the author's understanding of strength: rather than of being strong.

The extract on the next page is taken from:

"The Voice of Silence" by Oonagh Shanley Toffolo.

"A Strong Woman Verses a Woman of Strength:"

"A strong woman works out every day to keep her body in shape... but a woman of strength builds relationships to keep her soul in shape.

A strong woman isn't afraid of anything... but a woman of strength shows courage in the midst of fear.

A strong woman won't let anyone get the better of her... but the woman of strength gives the best of herself to everyone.

A strong woman makes mistakes and avoids the same in the future... A woman of strength realizes life's mistakes can also be unexpected blessings, and capitalizes on them.

A strong woman wears a look of confidence on her face... but a woman of strength wears grace.

A strong woman has faith that she is strong enough for the journey but the woman of strength has faith that it is in the journey that she will become strong."

(Anon)

The Goldfish That Jumped

The World Through My Eyes

"Slow down and enjoy life.
It's not only the scenery you miss by going too fast –
you also miss the sense of where you are going and why"

Eddie Cantor

Despite feeling suicidal about the relationship breakdown, the uncertainty of my future, how I could live with my failures as I saw them, at least. . . . my expectations and attachments to outcomes in life had not gone as I had wanted them to; I knew in my heart that I could never end my life – I have four beautiful children and could not have left them on the Earth Plane – motherless.

I had wanted the perfect marriage, the perfect relationship, the perfect life. I was 35 years old and really felt that I didn't know my life's purpose. I was completely lost in what seemed like a huge, vast ocean. A ship without a sail, directionless. Without hope or faith in my future and cast along with waves continually crashing and thrashing alongside. . . . the waves were slapping me into a state of awakening.

"A crisis event often explodes the illusions that anchor
our lives."
Robert Veninga.

So, I had NO choice and my inner journey began. After divorcing their father, he too was in a great deal of pain and he wouldn't help by sharing responsibility; financially, or physically by helping with the care of the children. I was on the hamster wheel, of work, sleep, work, sleep. I existed and was too tired to *enjoy* anything.

Working full-time in the Civil Service was taking its toll. I was regularly off sick – exhausted, tired and emotionally battered. There is a quote by Theodore Roethke "In a dark time, the eye begins to see".

Things had to change – I realized for the first time I had to create that change. No-one else. Just ME. I took great strength from looking and actually being PRESENT with my children, sitting and watching TV with them, enjoying them when we went walking into the local park, beach, etc.

The small things began to seem so much more important. I began to realize just how much strength they gave me and how much I had denied them by previously putting most of my energies into relationships. I began to realize how much I had actually denied MYSELF. I began to see that all my answers were here – here in these precious simple moments. "Beauty is Simple: Simplicity is Beauty."

I often cried, bursting into tears at the drop of a hat - during the day, and often at night, when alone. I felt exhausted with life. "Why me?" kept running like a stuck record through my mind. "How can I improve my life?" I prayed and although I felt some comfort in the connection, the only real connection came once I began to go WITHIN.

I took a long, hard, serious look at ME: What had brought me to this place? What had influenced me along the way? How often I had known my relationships would fail and yet still I'd gone into them - rushing in as fools do; only to fall flat on my face and end up broken – then to do it all again!

If we always do what we have always done, we will always get what we always got.

How absolutely true! The time for change was now – right here, right now, right this minute.

The Simplicity of Nurturing

"We achieve a sense of self from what we do for ourselves and how we develop our capacities. If all your efforts have gone into developing others you're bound to feel empty. TAKE YOUR TURN NOW"

Robin Norwood

I had never nurtured myself. Never even considered it to be a part of my life, life was just something to be "got on with". Having four children and a limited income restricted me in many ways. Over the coming months I decided I would make changes. "True Life is lived when tiny changes occur." Leo Tolstoy. Life for the goldfish was about to change.

I needed time. TIME TO HEAL AND TIME FOR ME. I needed to think about how to nurture myself, to change from the constant work, sleep, routine and to create those changes mindfully.

I began to connect with my inner self - MY SOUL.

What do I want from life?

Where do I want to be?

Surely there is more to life?

What are my long term plans?

Do I have any goals/aspirations?

What do I need to live a more satisfying, fulfilling life?

The Goldfish That Jumped

This Was All About Me

"The miracle comes quietly into the mind that stops an instant and is still"

A Course in Miracles

My ex partner introduced me to a dear friend; she was a Reiki Master and teacher. I had had several Reiki healing treatments with her before the relationship breakdown and I knew I needed to continue. She suggested I join her for T'ai Chi classes.

T'ai Chi is a gentle form of exercise, likened to martial arts in slow form. The stillness encourages the mind to be still too. Initially, my intention was to become fitter: little did I know that when I tuned into my heart, asking the question – 'did it feel right for me' that the resounding answer "Yes" would prove to be one of the most powerful, wondrous decisions I would ever make.

My first attendance at T'ai Chi was wonderful. Our teacher Janette, was very spiritual and became a great friend. At the time I failed to notice that she was psychic like me. I am eternally indebted to her. I was warmly welcomed into the group and found the exercises relatively easy. I began to "feel" different. T'ai Chi became a focus for me and provided me with inspiration from lots of like-minded people who encouraged me to grow and BE.

With each weekly session I felt an "inner knowing" that I had done this before. I felt very much at home with the other group members and was never judged, criticized or made to feel any different; despite being a newcomer. In fact, I felt I had known many of them for years. I now realise that we are soul companions and had lived together in communities before in past lives.

The T'ai Chi classes were held in what had been the school hall of my infant years. I was being taken on a journey back through my school life too. I had always been very happy there and had a wonderful teacher Mrs Robinson.

She had a beautiful, bright, golden energy field – I always felt loved and safe with her – wrapped in light and loveliness. A magical combination of fond memories of the old school days, and now, the experiences that would carry me into a whole new understanding of life. Now I was finding my spirituality: the journey into my heart and soul.

Over the coming months my soul expanded at an incredibly fast pace. Janette was a psychic like me and I decided to make an appointment for a reading. The date was 22nd July 2002; at the time I was not sure what I expected, I just followed a hunch that it was the right thing to do.

The information she gave me was incredibly detailed and accurate, relating to past, present and future. My past lives were also mentioned. She stated that I had been an Atlantean Priestess and this lifetime was about resolving the karma surrounding that time.

My children were mentioned and I was amazed with the accuracy of detail. She said that my daughter had been a dancer and an artist in her past lives. She is a wonderful dancer and artist in this lifetime too. My eldest son had been treated very badly and murdered by the Puritans in America. No wonder he didn't even like people mentioning the USA.

Her tone changed and she then asked if I had had a difficult labour and birth with my middle son. She enquired as to whether or not he had been a difficult baby and toddler too. I answered yes to all her questions; wondering where the conversation was leading.

She explained that he had been born with past life trauma. My middle son had had past lives in the concentration camps in Germany. His parents were very wealthy merchants, who had had everything stripped from them, before being captured and killed.

He and his little sister had been transferred to the concentration camps. He had become solely responsible for his little sister, until she eventually died in the camps. At this point, he had given up his will to live, and he too died of starvation. Another revelation, as he had a fascination with history of that time, and had achieved incredibly high grades through his school work relating to this subject of World War 2. He was not a child who loved to read books, yet, any on this subject would be thoroughly read, if not re-read.

My youngest son had just acquired an old desk from school. She described it exactly as it was and explained that in a previous life his uncle had made it for him. Once he reconnected with that energy he would and allow it to go and in turn would become more creative with projects including woodwork.

Very soon after I had had the reading, he obtained a place on a vocational course for building materials. He was incredibly successful and even won a prize representing the whole of Lancashire.

She said many things about me too; that I would benefit greatly from a deeper understanding of spiritual teachings relating to the spiritual laws. That by healing and nurturing my own heart centre, I would bring love into my life.

My karma would clear within the next 6-7 years, I had very little anyway. That I would teach again, as I once had in Atlantis and in many previous lifetimes. Travel was a huge feature too as part of this lifetime, again just as it had been in Atlantis.

She stated that I was a great healer, and that eventually people would heal, merely, from being in my presence alone. At the time

I did not understand much relating to that particular information. She said I would travel far and wide. That people would travel to visit me and that I would write books and sacred teachings.

During the session, I explained that I had a phobia of worms and she mentioned that this related to the dark conscience of mankind and I must bring that into the light. I was here to bring darkness to light. She also said that this lifetime is about abundance.

This reading was done over eight years ago. Whilst checking the detail of what was stated then, I am amazed to notice what has materialized. Although I include readings in my work, I never cease to be amazed by the information I am given in the readings relating to my clients. They return and confirm all that has happened it really is quite incredible.

Let The Magic Begin

"Beauty is eternity gazing at itself in a mirror.
But you are eternity and you are the mirror"

Kahlil Gibran

For the first time in my life I was beginning to respect and listen to my body. I realized I needed a rest and more likely a holiday, and, no doubt, so did my beloved children. Finances were tight and the fact that I had to manage four youngsters meant that visiting a foreign country was out of the question.

So, as a family we agreed, the lakes would be a great place to stay. I duly booked a family caravan and we set off. Each day we visited somewhere new - Hawkshead, Cartmel, Bowness. I was waking up - or rather re-awakening, and realizing I could do things. I had the POWER TO CHANGE MY LIFE MYSELF by making the right decisions, the journey had started and I was embracing it fully.

"I learned that nothing is impossible when we follow our inner guidance, even when its direction may threaten us by reversing our usual logic." Gerald Jampolsky.

Although I am psychic, I am unable to do readings for myself, very occasionally I hear voices (clairaudience), very, very occasionally I dream prophetically.

During the holiday we visited many Lakeland places of interest and in the remaining days of our holiday, we had planned to visit Dumfries, Derwent Water and Keswick. It was very difficult that day to make a decision about where to start.

We eventually settled on Dumfries, Scotland and enjoyed the sights of the city and a beautiful fried haggis. However, during the drive back to the caravan the children were very fractious. I was exhausted and being a single mother, I had no one with whom I could share the driving.

I was very tempted to return home to Lancashire but far too exhausted to drive further south than the Lakes. We were all fraught and short-tempered with one another. When we finally arrived, I sent them to bed and curled up in my space; angry and dishevelled. I could quite easily have walked away that evening, leaving the children behind.

That evening I dreamt of the most beautiful lake, which had a tangible magic. It was surrounded by mountains. The dream had amazing detail; I saw an old mansion, a boat yard, launch, an island with a house at the centre and I must admit when I awoke the following morning I was incredibly spaced out.

I must have had a grin like a Cheshire Cat for hours! The children asked me why I seemed so different; I recounted the dream and all the details to them clearly. I knew I was connected very powerfully to my soul. It felt that this place, wherever it was, was a most important part of the jigsaw......... I had no idea where it was; but knew it was certainly somewhere I needed to visit; assuming I could connect the pieces of the jigsaw together.

The following morning the children all apologized as we made up a picnic. We set off for Keswick, fully recharged and refreshed. We all loved the town and they treated themselves with their pocket money to various items of memorabilia. It was a truly remarkable, lovely day. The weather was lovely – a rarity, especially in the Lake District!

So, in true HAWORTH family style, my children and I had no intention of returning to the caravan before sundown. It was getting on for four pm as we trudged tiredly down towards the lake. Although Derwentwater is only a short journey from the town centre of Keswick we were all tired.

So, when I saw the sign advertising the launch, I thought it would be a lovely experience for the children to enjoy a boat ride; whilst at the same time, I could enjoy a REST!!! I purchased the tickets and we were all thrilled to be welcomed on a lovely old boat for a circular tour of the lake.

As the boat set off I remember vividly looking over all my children and feeling an immense love, joy and pride surge through my whole being. The feeling was for them as a family unit and also as individuals. A sense of peace rolled over me and it deepened as we moved out into the lake.

As the launch headed south towards Borrowdale, déjà vu slapped me in the face. I was dumb-struck and unable to speak or to move. I was oblivious to my surroundings; the children continued to chatter, ask questions; as children always do!

Emily, my daughter, realized something was different about me and tried to get my attention as I was unresponsive to them. Matthew soon followed and they both became a little concerned that I was transfixed and unable to answer.

The volume of their voices began to increase, and I recall clearly Emily looking at me, then realizing that I was overcome with the joy and awe of this magical place. "You're alright mum," she said "this is the place that you talked about in your dream isn't it?" Emily being Emily, quickly reassured her brothers: "She's okay, she's okay, it's that dream – the one she told us about yesterday, look at her face, look at her eyes, she's okay." I clearly remember her turning towards me and looking straight into my eyes – "Aren't you mum?"……….. "Yes." I replied, very quietly and reassuringly. I was silent for the rest of the journey, an energy surged through me that I had never previously felt.

I "knew" this place, I "knew" I belonged here and I "knew" I had to return, sooner, rather than later. The place consumed my soul and touched my whole being. It was a truly magical experience. At the end of the trip, I could just about manage to stand, and felt I floated off the boat on to the pier.

The children had never seen me so contented. I had never been so contented in my whole life either. That feeling is with me today and as I write this book it runs through me as powerfully as it did on that first day.......... this place is my haven. I accepted and allowed myself TO BE in awe and my space. My thoughts, and my presence, I feel now, were in fact changed that day; touched for the better throughout my whole soul.

I did not recognize then just how powerful Keswick and Derwentwater were to me and I certainly did not know how prominent they would BECOME in my life. Although my soul was definitely open, Derwentwater opened it further and was to become even more important in my "opening" process.

We left as dusk approached and a voice said "please come back as soon as you can". I was surprised and gently explained that with the combination of full-time employment, a limited budget, four children and a home to run that that may be a little difficult.

I knew I had to return to this magical place: so did the children.

Rebirth (Again)

"I learn by going where I have to go"

Theodore Roethke

By listening to my inner self I experienced a deeper knowing that Derwentwater and the surrounding areas were part of me. I was aware that by spending time in The Lakes this would really provide me with a spring board to allowing the opening and understanding of my soul.

I was now on a mission and I knew an opportunity would arise sooner, rather than later, for me to return. Within the week, the children, who all attended scouts, were invited to attend a camp at Bowness, in The Lake District.

It was very close to my birthday and, for my present my dear grandparents had given me some money. I was ***told*** to spend it on myself. Like most mothers, our children come first, and, any spare cash is spent on them. However, on this occasion I knew that I had to return to this place of wonder and awe, I was excited and nervous at the same time. A new level of me was about to emerge.

I had never been away from the children. I was, and still am a dedicated mother. Like a child taking her first steps tentatively, I asked my dad how I would find a bed and breakfast. I wasn't even aware that websites existed, to allow you to look online at hotels, lodges, etc.!

The Goldfish That Jumped

This really was a whole new experience for me. As we trawled through one bed and breakfast after another, I was in awe at the lovely decorated, homeliness of the wide ranging accommodation. Many were booked up for the Bank Holiday weekend, and I was just about to lose faith that I would find anything, when we found a really beautiful B & B, that was right in the centre of Keswick.

I jotted down the telephone number and dialled hoping to book the last room available. The landlady was very helpful, chatty and homely. She instantly made me feel at ease and I was duly booked in, directions were noted and I was told I was staying in the attic room. Fresh home-baked bread and jams would welcome me every morning and they looked forward to meeting me. No going back now! I was so excited I could have burst.

Nurturing myself was an entirely new concept for me. For the first time ever, I booked myself into a Bed & Breakfast in Keswick. I enjoyed spending the money on myself and it was the start of a huge adventure.

The children would be on camp from Friday evening to Monday: three precious days to MYSELF. It was a great feeling, though I confess, I hadn't been away from them before and I was a little apprehensive. Nonetheless I was certainly determined that I was going to have a great time.

I was really excited, time to myself to enjoy the scenery and relax. A whole weekend to myself: it was a very exciting prospect. This was a new experience which I had created, now I was beginning to live whole-heartedly.

I finished work, fed the children and tidied around. We loaded the car and set off on our big adventure. I love driving up the M6 motorway to The Lakes; there is a sense of rejuvenation and peacefulness the further north you journey. We arrived at the scout camp and I was thrilled that their list of activities was going to keep them very busy.

The Goldfish That Jumped

As I drove off, I knew I could relax in the knowledge that they would be taken care of by scout masters who had become very good friends. The drive between Bowness and Keswick is about an hour. It was a drive of peacefulness to me.

I was about to be spoilt, to be allowed to do what I wanted, when I wanted. I had no responsibilities other than to myself. Well deserved respite after years of caring for children, day after day. The journey was full of beautiful scenery, a lovely spring evening and I easily located my delightful B & B.

I settled in a beautiful attic room and made myself a cuppa. As I drank my tea I took in all the details of the room and its decor. It was decorated with blue and white wallpaper, matching bedding and furnishings; very beautiful and homely.

I felt like a queen, in her palace and was looking forward to enjoying every single, precious moment of the weekend. I couldn't wait to get to the Lake again and be touched by the magnificence of the water, the mountains and the ambience of the setting.

After drinking my cuppa, I freshened up and promptly set off. It was approaching dusk and there was a most lovely sunset. The sunsets in this magical place brighten the mountains. The skylines are always awesome and inspirational. My soul was being touched with magic again, and, it was opening to receive all the beauty, that this wonderful place was offering to me.

On the lake a boat had been decorated with beautiful fresh flowers, for a wedding which was about to take place. I was really touched and sent a quiet prayer, for a successful, loving marriage for the happy couple. A thought passed through my head that maybe, just maybe, I would meet someone special and re-marry. What a perfect setting and perfect start to their married life.

I wandered for quite a while by the lakeside. I was aware light was fading so knew I couldn't stay for as long as I would have liked. The excitement of knowing that I would awaken here tomorrow and the following day were just fabulous. I felt as though I would burst with excitement and happiness. All that existed was me and this place of joyousness.

I eventually sauntered back to the B & B. As I got ready for bed I realized how tired I was and soon drifted off into a deep sleep. The following morning I awoke fresh and with a stillness and joy in my soul.

Breakfast was fabulous, a range of fruit, home-made bread and best of all – I HADN'T LIFTED A FINGER. Pure bliss, no cooking, no washing up, no ironing and no children!!! Although I had visited Keswick once before, I wasn't familiar with the area and decided that I would purchase a local guide book, listing all the local walks.

Whilst in the hiking shop, I asked the owners advice regarding walks and beauty spots. They were very helpful and from there I walked down to the lake again and fed the ducks. The weather was warm and sunny; I really was being spoilt by The Universe. Although I was in The Lakes, there was not a spot of rain in sight!

I looked through the books and decided my first visit would be to the church at St. John in the Vale. Tomorrow I and would visit the stone circle at Castlerigg. I experienced déjà vu everywhere I went, in the church, when I stood on the mountain tops and even recollected memories of living in a house by the waterside. It was awesome, everything, my soul felt like it belonged here and I was struck with a feeling of belonging. Yet, here I was alone and in a strange place. How could this be?

Despite frequent thoughts of the children, and of course checking my mobile phone – just in case, I knew they were fine and thanked those who had given their time to providing this special opportunity, to all the participating children and the parents who had a chance of change.

New Beginnings & Castlerigg

"He who binds to himself a joy
Does the winged life destroy:
But he who kisses the joy as it flies
Lives in eternity's sun rise"

William Blake "Eternity"

The following morning I promptly set off early for the stone circle; Castlerigg. The town was quiet as it was so early and there was an ambience of peace and tranquillity. I felt very contented within myself and felt a peace inside which I had never experienced before.

The guidebook was easy to understand; just as well as my map reading skills have been questioned before! I wandered up the road leading up to the stone circle. The scenery was magnificent. I was surrounded by mountains, the Skiddaw range and could see the peaks, Cat Bells and Walla Crag, which reached above the lake. It was a steep climb, so my pace was slowed. I peered over the hedgerow towards Blencathra mountain, otherwise known as Saddle-Back.

In the next field was a newly-born calf; the umbilical cord was still attached and steam was evaporating from his tiny form. His mother looked warily at me and I was really touched to witness and be present in this precious moment. I thought of the significance of the new birth; of this beautiful calf, and the rebirth that I was experiencing. I was letting go of my old self, the old hurt, the constant tiredness and stresses. Now I was welcoming in the new and the lovely. The goldfish was allowing and experiencing joy in my life for the first time.

I sent a huge prayer of thanks up to The Universe.

I continued my walk and entered the field where the circle is located. As I neared Castlerigg, I was amazed and I felt an immediate connection. The surrounding mountainous views were spectacular. I was so thrilled, tears ran down my cheeks. I felt like I had come home, I belonged in this place and "knew" it in my soul. My whole being was overcome with JOY.

As it was so early in the morning, no one else was about, which meant that I could fully embrace this place without any distractions. The feelings I experienced of that very first visit to such a magical and inspirational place, have stayed with me to this day. I stayed for some time, touching each of the stones, walking around the circle clockwise, then in an anti-clockwise direction. Peace ran through each and every cell in my body.

The feeling that I have returned home always runs through me in a most beautiful, contented way. I have revisited it many times, occasionally with friends and often alone. In fact, more recently, I have done much healing work up there. Castlerigg touched my soul and many who have visited with me say they certainly feel some connection.

The weekend brought an absolute peace to my soul. I now knew that if ever I felt sad or down, in any way, all I would have to do would be to think of this place, look through the photographs, meditate on it and my wholeness would be restored. The whole area had touched my soul and uplifted me. I received a healing that was so powerful; I had been given the strength to go on with my life's journey, knowing that all was indeed, as it should be.

I decided to journey over to St John in the Vale church from the stone circle. The whole trip was several miles and I knew in my soul I had to visit this little chapel. The views were stunning and again I felt I knew this place too. As I opened the little doorway and ventured in I knew I had been here before. I knew I had been married here and had also been buried here too.

By now, there was such a deepening, a linking of all the threads of the connections, that I knew I would continue to return time, and time again. I knew that each occasion I returned, I would be touched and my soul would expand its awareness. I had a deep knowing that, if I ever needed guidance, or diving inspiration, this was the place of magic. I was spellbound to return.

My last night in the B & B was wonderful and being spoilt for breakfast another joy. I was looking forward to seeing the children and at the same time, sad to be leaving. After breakfast I packed, settled the bill and ventured down to the lake to say my own private goodbye. I gave thanks for all I had experienced, and all that this wonderful place had allowed me to feel.

I knew I had changed profoundly that weekend and knew that life had to return to normal. Yet, the deep sense of calm and peace I carried, meant that I was so connected there was very little sadness. I knew I would have opportunity to return soon, and I knew my heart and soul, would guide me, as to when and this deepened my acceptance and understandings.

Later, after lunch, I set off south to collect the children. They'd had a wonderful time too and were all happy to see me. Travelling home in the car it was obvious that we were all refreshed and rejuvenated. They commented on how different I looked and seemed. I smiled a contented smile that ran through the whole of my being.

The Goldfish That Jumped

Jet Propulsion

*"All you need to do to receive guidance
is to ask for it and then listen"*

Sanaya Roman

Being in the presence of those who have open hearts, and thus lovely bright, light energy fields was a joyful experience. Being around those who attended T'ai Chi brought this to me weekly. I continued to enjoy the classes and also practiced at home. T'ai Chi daily, just 5 or 10 minutes, made so much difference to the way in which my day started.

I was FINDING ME and actually finding, day by day, that I was becoming happy IN ME; something I had never felt before, nor understood, nor even considered. I love this quote from "Auguries of Innocence" by William Blake *"To see a world in a grain of sand, And heaven in a wild flower. Hold Infinity in the palm of your hand, And eternity in an hour"*.

I was beginning to listen, understand and "know" my soul - my inner-self.

The more I listened to my body, rested and learnt not to push too hard, the more the changes IN ME began to show themselves on the physical levels. My periods became less painful, my asthma attacks became less frequent and I no longer had the need for my inhalers. I began to breathe in life. My migraines became less acute and, rather than lasting for days, they were only lasting for a few hours. I took less and less medication, and, thankfully had fewer and fewer trips to the doctors too.

I felt empowered and started to change my life. I began a night school course in counselling. My hope, my long term plan was to leave the Civil Service and do something where I would experience job satisfaction. Maybe, even at this stage in my life, I knew I was to leave the Civil Service.

For the first time ever I was looking at my long term future. I thought about my pension and was concerned about government pension provision. I decided to make enquiries to move my pension into a private company, and duly called my financial advisor Marcus White. Marcus and I had known one another for almost 10 years. Over the years, he had sorted out life insurance and endowment policies. I certainly trusted him to sort out my civil service pension.

As I dialled the numbers, I thought back to the very first time I had heard his voice, the familiarity of it. I was sure I had heard it before. Then, when we had met all those years ago, there did indeed, seem something so comfortable and familiar to me relating to him.

He was delighted to hear from me, as always, and he made arrangements regarding the necessary paperwork, in order that I could change my pension. He forwarded it for me to sign. I was tiling the bathroom that weekend, therefore planned to read it on the Sunday evening.

Marcus called me on Saturday evening to ask what I was doing. I explained I had not read the literature, relating to the pension, and I was covered in paint and tile adhesive. Being a little dumb (and very slow!) I hadn't realised where the conversation was going. "Can you be ready in an hour?" "Why?" I asked stupidly. "Because I am taking you out, can you get a baby sitter?"

Marcus was a very wealthy man and I knew he would treat me well. Whilst getting ready, I recognised that at previous times, I would have felt I didn't deserve, and couldn't possibly go out with a man like this. So, I recognised I had moved forward and duly got myself dolled up. Mum kindly agreed to babysit.

The Goldfish That Jumped

He arrived early in his BMW sports car and when he saw me, he had a huge grin which stretched, from ear to ear. He hugged me tightly, and it was obvious he was delighted to see me. He asked where I would like to dine, and we journeyed to a very expensive Indian restaurant. I was treated like a lady for the whole evening. This was nothing less than I deserved, but something I had NEVER allowed in my life previously, because I had believed I was not worthy!

We arrived back at Marcus' lovely cottage quite late, and we talked while he made coffee. He openly admitted his feelings for me, explaining that he had fallen in love with me the very first time he met me, almost ten years before. At that time, both he and I were married, so neither of us were in a position to follow our feelings.

I remembered how comfortable and safe I felt in his presence that very first time I met him, and how he touched my soul at the time, and how, each time I saw him, our friendship had blossomed. He bowled me over by his honesty and I laughed saying "You are messing about." His eyes told a different story.

The love was deep and heartfelt. I felt a connection here I had never felt before. We kissed and I remembered our first meeting, how we met, how I had known his voice on the phone the very first time I had heard it. How deeply he looked into my eyes on our first meeting. Here we were – almost ten years later in one another's arms and all the hurt that we had both been through following both marital break downs was dissolving.

How strange life is at times – how we hide our feelings – yet here I was recollecting those memories as powerful as ever they were, all those years before.

Although neither of us wanted to part, my family commitments were paramount in our minds. Marcus drove me home and we agreed to meet again soon. Our second meeting was just as magical and we shared much.

The Goldfish That Jumped

Marcus asked if I would like to borrow Shirley MacLaine's book, "Out on a Limb". I agreed I would like to and began to read about this wonderful lady and her wonderful life – and her journey inward to her SOUL. Reading the book certainly sent my soul into jet propulsion. Shirley MacLaine's book further opened my soul – in it she discusses her experiences of déjà vu. I read the book although, at that time, my understanding was limited.

The Wow Factor

"The most beautiful thing we can experience is the mysterious"

Albert Einstein

And then................... it happened!!

Whilst walking in the local country park, I "felt" different, as I walked down a small hill. I "saw" Marcus in front of me wearing clothing, rather like hessian sack. It was as if someone were showing a film or play. The pictures were very clear, despite not being "solid". I have never smoked cigarettes, taken drugs or done anything of that nature. I have only ever been drunk three times in my whole life – despite this I questioned what I had eaten and done that morning – nothing out of the ordinary – I hadn't even had a paracetamol!!!

I was gobsmacked; no one was around, yet it was as though a movie was playing right before my eyes. I wondered if I was going insane and I checked if I could feel my legs and my feet. I felt my face too; all were intact.

As I continued to walk, I watched the pictures change to include me too. I was also dressed in clothing you would associate with medieval times. Marcus, this time, stumbled into the second picture and was obviously, very seriously injured. I felt, and knew, I was his wife. He had a spear through his left shoulder and septicaemia was setting in.

A deep knowing swept over me, that he was the leader of our village. He had travelled to battle, as our village was being threatened by a war lord. The men fought alongside him, and, although they had managed to protect the village, for a while longer at least, they were all exhausted; weakened after their traumas in battle. They had journeyed far, and it had taken over a week for them to return to the village. The injury Marcus had sustained, in the last battle, had worsened throughout the homeward journey.

Despite my healing, my knowledge as a medicine woman of our peoples, and my caring for my beloved Marcus, hours later, he died in my arms. The journey back from the battle field had taken its toll; it was too little, too late. The vision showed us in the thatched round house. Later, I heard my agonizing screams, as the realisation, that I was now a widow, raged through me. From childhood, my ultimate fear in this life time, was, that I would be a widow.

The feelings were very powerful and I was feeling shocked, stunned and actually very scared. I remember sitting on the nearest bench by the brook and trying to gather my thoughts. The vision was to my left, and from where I was now sitting, it was behind me. I turned back to look, and each time I did, the vision of the house remained.

Tears rolled down my cheeks, I couldn't get Marcus out of my head and I felt feelings I had never felt before. I still questioned whether or not I was going insane, though could still feel my physical body and knew I hadn't died nor was I having an out of body experience, such as astral projection. What had just happened?

I sat on the bench for quite some time. I could not understand what had occurred and for some reason, I was afraid for Marcus too. It took me quite some time, to gather enough strength to walk the rest of the distance to the car. A quote by Theodore Roethke comes to mind: "What shakes the eye but the invisible." I was thoroughly shaken, right to my core.

As the images replayed through my mind, I knew I had to talk to Marcus. I immediately called him when I got home, disappointed and frustrated, when his answer machine message explained he was on holiday.

He had mentioned he would be going skiing with his sons. I took a note of the return date, eager to check on his welfare. Several days later he called me. As we spoke, upon his return, I was most surprised to hear that, during the holiday, he had had a skiing accident. He needed emergency surgery to his left shoulder: which had been pinned together.

I was most surprised and suggested we meet up soon. He agreed and we arranged to meet a few days later. He had cooked a lovely meal and I was really moved to see him. However, though I felt this way, our next meeting was somewhat different. He seemed closed and he explained he was in financial straits and had a number of personal issues which, over the coming months, would need his close care and attention. He apologised for his detached manner.

I tried desperately to make sense of it all. I had never experienced anything like this. To me at that time, it was a pivotal point in my life. I was desperate to explain the pictures. Why he had lent me the book? Why he had told me of his deepest feelings for me? And yet here he was, almost broken? It all seemed very peculiar and had left me in a state of confusion. Had he experienced déjà vu? Why had he fallen in love with me the first time we met? I had so many questions and NO answers.

My search was becoming a mission for a deepened understanding of what I had experienced, and what I desperately wanted to understand. I was becoming more aware by the day and wanted someone to explain what was happening. I just wanted answers to all the weird instances that were happening to me.

Marcus called me a few days later to say that he did not want me to be dragged into his personal affairs. He could not cope with the thought of pulling me down, and being upset by everything, that he was going through. He suggested that we should take a break from the relationship. He apologised profusely, and was obviously very saddened by his decision. I heard from him less and less frequently, and, over time he faded into the background. We didn't date again.

Even now, when I see him, his eyes still hold the love – its mutual – always will be. Maybe he was there to re-awaken a part of me? At the time it was very hard to live without that contact. Now I realize that he came to open a part of my heart, and my soul to a deepened level of understanding. The flame allowing me to experience my past life déjà vu had been reignited; the full understanding would take much longer.

We cannot run before we can walk…….. no matter how much we would like to!!!

I hold his memories as dear to my heart and my soul, because he provided it with a massive forward push. He apologised several months later, explaining he had been in a dark shadowy place, the dark night of the soul. He'd experienced great financial loss; almost bankruptcy, his sons were causing great concern, as was his ex-wife. He hadn't wanted to drag me down to that place.

I will always honour what Marcus provided for me on my journey and I often think kindly thoughts of him.

The Journey Continues

"Until we accept the fact that life itself is founded in mystery, we shall learn nothing."

Henry Miller

This had been one of my first traumatic experiences of past lives. I admit that if anyone had broached the subject previously, I had been totally dismissive. My thirst for knowledge was growing by the day and as I had gained so much from Shirley MacLaine's book I plumped to buy "The Camino".

If "Out on a Limb" got me started, "The Camino" provided much more of the same. The Camino is a pilgrimage between France and Spain which Shirley MacLaine journeyed. Despite being a celebrity, she did not stay in expensive hotels, she chose to experience The Camino as all others pilgrims do. In fact, some nights she slept out in the open. It is her story of how things unfolded, of how she was touched by experiences; much relating to her personal déjà vu. She tapped into a deeper knowing and often "saw" pictures and spirits along the way.

In the book, she explains her experiences of her past lives, whilst on the pilgrimage and relates them to what had happened in this lifetime too. The book is written with sincerity, real depth, and strength of emotion. It made me realise that I wasn't the only person on the planet to witness, and to experience the power of déjà vu. Maybe I wasn't going crazy after all. This was just what I needed, to provide me with the impetus, to continue my search towards a bigger, much deeper understanding.

I experienced more flash backs – some with Marcus, some with others, and I began to tap into a much deeper knowing – of myself. My inner trust within grew and my instincts sharpened. I learnt to accept the process and actually embraced it, rather than allowing the fear of what was happening to consume my being.

Around the same time, I was experiencing frequent déjà vu of Atlantis. I remembered being a priestess, teaching spiritual lessons, assisting children and new mothers. I loved my work and my peoples. Atlantis was a most peaceful, welcoming community; some would perhaps compare it to Heaven.

The community of Atlantis was based on an island which I knew to be Hawaii. We used natural healing methods and many, many crystals. In fact, we had beds made out of crystals, which we would lie upon to recharge our batteries and balance the chakras. Most were made of rose quartz. The peace of the whole island was a pleasure to experience and remains a tangible feeling to this day.

However, in our sacred teachings, known only to a select few, it was written that Atlantis would be destroyed. This would be necessary as the introduction of science and genetic modification would lead to the detachment from Source. The soulful lives we had led would be phased out and the teachings of energy work and energy management would be eradicated.

The focus of respect would be totally towards the scientists, their works in explaining how mankind came to be in existence, and how much control they could have over the true powers of nature. In my heart and soul, my whole being, I knew these ancient teachings were correct and embraced daily what I had, rather than focusing on what was to come. That was a beautiful pleasant lifetime that I recalled easily. Further details of the extent of déjà vu of that time would unfold years later.

More Jigsaw Pieces

*"If you want to succeed in the world
you must make your own opportunities."*

John B. Gough

I was certainly on my path – I continued with the T'ai Chi, having Reiki treatments and was blessed to meet lots of new people and friends. I realize now that my soul had advanced, my aura was more open and brighter, so, I was attracting in to my life my soul companions.

Often we have lived in communities with like-minded people. Once we regain that level of inspiration or soulfulness that we lived with then, we automatically attract and fit in to the soul group again. Hence most of my dear friends are healers.

Many have experienced their own process of déjà vu. They know their past lives, have an understanding of who they have been and many of them know who I am. Often we communicate through the mind, without the need for physical speech and embrace our inner knowing.

As my intuition deepened, my soul expanded and I became more and more aware of my life. How I had affected my own process and, as a consequence, I began to take control. I looked at how I had actually caused much of my own unhappiness. My inward journey was about MY PERSONAL RESPONSIBILITY TO MYSELF. All I had created was indeed, of my own creation. This was both a powerful and painful realization.

Asking for help from The Universe through prayer and thought was very personal to me. This meant that, day by day, the picture unfolded. I began to read books on spirituality by authors like Doreen Virtue, Rosemary Altea, Diana Cooper, Hazel Raven, Jack Kornfield and many others. The books confirmed my knowing and many authors mentioned details of Atlantis, much as I had pictured it. All the threads of the spider's web were beginning to join. I was realizing that as we touch one of the threads of the web, the vibration is felt somewhere else along its matrix.

I continued to enjoy T'ai Chi and to receive Reiki healing treatments from Tina Hill. She advised me to become a Reiki healer and I stated it wasn't for me, time and time again. Looking back now I can see how ridiculous that was, hindsight is a wonderful thing! I had a golden opportunity to learn Reiki and refused.

Little did I know at the time, how much the Reiki would allow me to grow and blossom. Tina suggested she could train me, although she had a feeling that it would be better for me if I trained with Liam. He was a dear friend of hers.

A few weeks later we all attended an Energy Workshop together and got on famously. He agreed to teach me Reiki, although we never managed to sort out the right timing. Either I was busy, or he was too busy. However, Liam did teach me many things about past lives in a short space of time.

He had been my brother in Atlantis which became very clear when I did a psychic reading for him. I charged him £10 and learnt a valuable lesson. He stated firmly and clearly that I gave as good a reading, and in fact, better than many other psychics and unless I charged, what they charged, I would be rubbished. I was learning self-value. He explained how we had both been Buddhist monks in past lives and as such had signed karmic contracts of poverty.

These contracts no longer served me and I was advised to sever them immediately. I needed abundance and I needed to learn how to welcome it in. This has been a very dear and difficult lesson indeed for me to learn and is about understanding what we deserve which is often about self-love, self-regard and self-esteem.

If I didn't feel I deserved better, then surely no-one else would either. I had experienced great poverty bringing up four children with a limited budget and no maintenance. I had created this for myself. I now needed to create and welcome in the change. I had to learn to welcome and engage in abundance. I was on a journey understanding about abundance in all aspects of life, health, wealth, peace, love and other beautiful life qualities.

The Goldfish That Jumped

Deepening Wisdom

"My job here on earth is twofold.
My job is first of all to make amends.
My second job is to awaken people who might be asleep.
Almost everyone is asleep!
THE ONLY WAY I CAN AWAKEN THEM
IS TO WORK ON MYSELF."

Dr. Ihaleakala Hew Len

This means that we take total, absolute responsibility for all we create and have created already in our lives. Everything we have in our lives we have attracted. It is a very, very powerful thought and indeed a very powerful truth. I was beginning to realise, recognise and actually understand how I had created my own living nightmare and. . . . realised now that I had control to change my destiny and LIVE. I had to create this change. I had to be the change. I knew I had to be and embrace inner change too.

By attending the energy workshop, T'ai Chi and having Reiki healing treatments, I was becoming even more aware of energies. I was more aware of what I focused on, as I could see that that is what I had manifested. Personal responsibility was becoming second nature to me in my everyday life.

As my knowledge deepened, I became aware of the Chakras. Chakra is a Sanskrit word for spinning wheel. They are energy wheels within the body. Chakras can also be photographed using the Kirlian energy cameras mentioned earlier. We are spiritual beings having a human experience. Therefore we need a means by which the soul can anchor into the body.

The chakras all need to spin in harmony and be balanced. There are 9 main energy vortexes in the body. They are located at various positions on the body: the base, located at the coccyx of the spine; the sacral centre, located near the navel; the solar plexus, located just below the breasts; the heart centre, located around the heart; the thymus, between the heart and the throat; the throat centre, located on the throat; the brow, located between the eyes; the crown, which is just above the head; then the upper crown, just above the first crown centre.

They circulate energy (chi) and allow energy to flow freely. When they are all perfectly synchronized the body is healthy and we are balanced mentally, emotionally, physically and spiritually. As with all things in life, we can adjust to a point whenever there is an imbalance, although when there is a major imbalance then we may feel very ill and/or out of sorts. For this reason all alternative/complementary therapies are aware of and treat the chakras.

Have you ever considered why someone has lots of pathology in a particular part of their body? A sore back, painful legs, sciatica and/or constipation, would signify to an energy worker that the base centre is misaligned. By treating and rebalancing this energy vortex, then recovery will commence.

We are energy beings and as such, we receive and transmit energies all the time. The heart centre is the main chakra and it is from here that we pick up other peoples energies and feelings. This is the point at which we begin to comprehend love, total unconditional love, self-love, self-regard and self-esteem, compassion, empathy and all the positive qualities of being a balanced, loving person.

The heart is where we feel energies the most, someone is thinking about us, someone welcomes us into their group or likewise when someone doesn't like us. Other examples include when we know a person is definitely not interested in us enough to commence a relationship or the point at which we know that they, or us, feel the relationship has ended. How often have you said or heard others say things like "I just don't feel I love you anymore".

We have all heard of someone who has been married very happily for years, one of the couple passes away and the other dies of a broken heart very soon afterwards. A broken heart is indeed what they have died of; as the energy in the heart centre has broken and the wheel has stopped spinning.

When one energy wheel ceases, the links with the other centres are broken, energy does not flow, the bodies systems break down. The energy is stagnant and becomes polluted and stuck. Eventually the lack of energy means that the physical body stills itself and death occurs as a result of lack of energy movement.

We cannot survive without energy in motion. Emotions are E(energy) in motion. By understanding these concepts we begin to understand the simplicity of the body. The emotions give us the emotional charge to create change, send love, healing and compassion to someone else, etc. How often do we meet someone and we just intuit that they quite like us, that they may fancy us? They have merely glanced at us across a crowded room, maybe smiled.

How do we pick up and interpret these feelings? We intuit and feel these vibrations through the heart centre. We may even be thinking of someone and they then telephone us or we may get a letter from them. There are many scientific experiments which prove this fact.

The DVD "The Living Matrix" is truly fascinating. It confirms much of what I have felt throughout my life. For me it also confirms that what I teach is the Truth – the true knowing that lies in each of us at our core: at our soul centre. We have wisdom and knowledge within ourselves, we just need to learn to tune into it more frequently and more easily.

The chakras spin at different rates; Gaia spins at 7.56Hz per second, so the base centre, located at the base of the spine rotates at between 7.56Hz and 7,500Hz per second. When this energy vortex is spinning at the right speed then we would say someone is grounded and balanced. A good example I often use to explain about energy movement is to liken it to water movement.

When water moves freely the energy in the water is balanced and wildlife can thrive. When the water becomes stagnant nothing can survive in that environment, it begins to smell foul and fish and wildlife die. Would you even consider drinking water from a stagnant pond?

Just because we do not always see energies, doesn't mean that we don't feel them. Each chakra is linked to a gland, part of the endocrine system, so when there is an emotional charge, fear for example, the vortex spins more rapidly and our bodies systems change. The "Fight or Flight" of adrenaline rush is a good example of energy in motion. When we are in the initial stages of love, the being in love stage, then we radiate huge amounts of love from the heart centre.

Unconditional love is by far the most powerful emotion that we can experience as human beings.

The Power and Memory of Water

"Water has a memory
and carries within it thoughts and prayers.
As you yourself are water, no matter where you are,
your prayers will be carried to the rest of the world."

Masaru Emoto

Masaru Emoto has studied water for several years now and is well respected in his field. Water carries memories and he studies crystals produced from water samples that have been exposed to different emotions and environments.

Water exposed to positive emotions such as love, compassion, gratitude, appreciation, joy, beauty produces wonderful, beautiful and perfect crystals. Water exposed to negative emotions, such as jealousy, anger, frustration, sadness, grief, etc. produces broken, disjointed crystals.

Maybe the aura reflects the bodies' water systems? Clear water in the body would be reflected in a clear, bright, light energy field. I often wonder is this why I see dark colours in the aura and know that that person has lots of emotional trauma and hurt.

Perhaps we could liken that to our bodies' water systems being polluted. This would also explain why, when we are working through old emotions, that we often seem to detoxify our body and drink and obviously urinate more frequently. Perhaps this is also why, as a healer I now drink far more water than I ever used to do.

97

In his many works, Emoto takes samples of water from a wide variety of sources. Water taken from a tap, especially London tap water, has much less vitality than that taken from a mountain stream. In comparison water taken from a tap in the Lake District is reasonably pure. Water taken from a natural lake rather than a man made reservoir also shows much more vitality.

As human beings, we are made up of approximately 70% water, the same percentage approximately as Mother Earth. Do you think that it would follow that the clearer, and less polluted the water we put into our bodies, so the clearer our thought processes. It has been proven that many children whilst at school who become 1% dehydrated, even before the feeling of thirst is stimulated, cannot concentrate as effectively.

Taking this one step further still, relating this back to Emoto's work. If water holds memories and we as human beings carry memories in our bodies' water systems then surely if we are exposed to negative emotions, belittling comments, criticisms, etc., our water is effectively polluted.

Psychologists now recognise that encouragement and positive feedback are a far more powerful tool which can be used when teaching and encouraging children to learn. Each of us as adults, are more likely, and willing to help someone with a positive attitude, rather than those with a negative and unappreciative nature. Maybe, this also explains the Buddhist concept of mindfulness and karma. Thinking positively and being mindful of our actions, taking personal responsibility for our thoughts, words and deeds could actually have a scientific validation?

Emoto's works are published by Beyond Words Publishing Inc. The statement of declared values is; "We give to all of life as life has given us. We honour all relationships. Trust and stewardship are integral to fulfilling dreams. Collaboration is essential to create miracles. Creativity and aesthetics nourish the soul. Unlimited thinking is fundamental. Living your passion is vital. Joy and humour open our hearts to growth. It is important to remind ourselves of love".

In general terms the larger, lighter and brighter the aura the better that person at having mastered humanitarian qualities. They are usually a being at peace with themselves and with others. When all the chakras are balanced this too is reflected in the aura. This would be representative of someone who is at peace.

Someone who is tuned in to their soul and who is honouring their life's purpose has a lovely, bright aura. These people are usually most happy and loving, a pleasure to be around and are usually healthy too.

They live from the soul, being non-judgemental and offering encouragement and support to those around them. They encourage and empower people and offer endearing qualities to ALL, even those whom others would reject or dismiss. Their qualities include naturally seeing the potential and goodness in others, in a balanced and healthy way. They are able to be firm but fair and assertive, without being aggressive.

We are all "a work in progress", I include myself here too, by aiming to be pure of heart and soul then it is reflected in the aura. I encourage those I meet to live from their heart centres. To make decisions from their heart centre; through here we can tune in to our soul and begin to have a deeper understanding of all that is.

I have yet to meet someone who is living from their soul who is not in touch with their heart-centre. As far as I am aware, if we are not connected to our heart-centre, we cannot be connected to our soul. Each one of us has all the answers inside ourselves, if we only take the time to listen.

By listening to the heart centre, we become more aware of our conditioning, through society and religion, cultural differences, etc. As we listen to our hearts, we realise and recognise, our own inner truth, and, we begin a process of letting go of old, worn out thinking patterns.

The Goldfish That Jumped

A most beautiful quote comes to mind:

"The things you believe in are the baggage you carry with you in your life. The true sage believes in nothing, other than the sacredness of all things. He lives in spontaneity of energy. He defends nothing nor judges anything. His world is eternal and infinite, he sees beauty in all things and he accepts the ways of man, including restriction and strife. He knows that without constraints there would be no challenges."

Stuart Wilde.

Manifestation Work

*"A rock pile ceases to be a rock pile the moment
a single man contemplates it,
bearing within him the images of a cathedral."*

Antoine de Saint – Exupery

Meditation is a great tool to help assist in this process, as is T'ai Chi/yoga, etc. By spending time listening to our Inner Self, listening to the pull of the soul, knowing when we need to change occupations, visit or call a friend or relative, take time to visit Mother Earth, etc., we become whole-hearted beings.

We are spiritual beings having a human experience. Most of us at one time or another are human beings DOING, rather than being. We are so wrapped up in everyday life and busy schedules that we live without thought to the long-term welfare of our souls' well-being. This is why many who find the spiritual path, often find it after being burnt out, ill or emotionally battered.

During the dark night of the soul, often following times when we are being so pulled and distant from our soul that the elastic band snaps. Soulfulness, awareness of our spirit and our truth, finally returns to its original shape and size, after being pulled in the opposite direction. How often we listen to our intuition or inner self is individual to us all. The more we listen, the more aware we become.

Every day is a conscious choice. Do we live from the heart centre or from the head? Do we combine both? There are times when we need to be in perfect balance and live from both the heart and the mind too. We can become more soulful and become more aware of our souls' needs. We now live in a very busy world and one where demands on our time are many and varied. By making time for yourself, you can change your rock pile into something really beautiful. What would you like to create? How would you like to restructure your life?

Through meditation, when we clear our thoughts and allow inspiration to come to the forefront, we can often use our creative minds to show us images of places we haven't visited for a while, or of loved ones. Often, during meditation we see through a new perspective and begin to change our lives.

Everything starts with a thought. An architect has a thought about the design of a house and draws up the plans. Within a short period of time, that house is built. Whatever you would like to change or improve in your life will start with a thought. Meditation is about listening and interpreting these thoughts.

A Deepening of Respect

"The art of living is neither careless drifting on the one hand nor fearful clinging on the other. It consists in being sensitive to each moment, in regarding it as utterly new and unique, in having the mind open and wholly receptive."

Alan Watts

Living a life in balance with all things is essential to our well-being. Living with our intuition and without strong rules/regulations and religious dogma will encourage and maintain this balance. The Native American Indians and other cultures demonstrated their connectedness to Mother Earth by showing compassion and respect for each other and every living thing around them. They respected the wisdom of the elders and passed that wisdom and knowledge down to their sons and daughters and grandchildren.

They had great medicine men and women, great shamans who were capable of healing themselves and others. The shamans were revered and respected in these cultures. They could heal the earth and bring rain, wind and sun. They could send energy to crops and livestock. When they chanted together or sent healing collectively their power was increased. It was only ever used for the highest good for all concerned.

The film "Avatar" is a wonderful depiction of these abilities and the ancient wisdom; the connectedness of the trees, the "Tree of Souls" and how each of them was connected to the other Avatar, to their animals and every living creature.

The Buddhist concept that we are all one is exactly what this means in real terms. As we help and assist others so we help and assist ourselves. The more openly we show qualities of humanitarianism the more it is shown to us.

Buddha, Jesus Christ, His disciples and other spiritual teachers, teach about compassion and enlightenment/heaven.

"He who wants to be great must become the smallest of all"
> Mark. 9. 35

"Whosoever exalts himself shall be abased: and he that humbles himself shall be exalted."
> Luke 18. 9-14

"You shall love your neighbour as yourselves."
> Mark 12. 31

"Hard it is to understand; by giving away our food, we get more strength: by bestowing clothing on others, we gain more beauty; by founding abodes of purity and truth we acquire great treasures. The charitable man has found the path of liberation. He is like the man who plants a sapling securing thereby the shade, the flowers and the fruit in future years. Even so is the result of charity, even so is the joy of him who helps those that are in need of assistance: even so is the great nirvana." Buddha.

"Spiritual truth is a truth of the spirit, not a truth of the intellect, not a mathematical theorem or a logical formula."

Sri Aurobindo

"There is a growing interest among the scientific community in Buddhist philosophical thought. I am optimistic that over the next few decades there will be a great change in our worldview both from the material and the spiritual perspectives."

The Dalai Lama.

Notice how similar these teachings are in making us aware of heart-centred energies. Yet, many religions teach dogma (rules) rather than Truths. Teachings of gratitude and appreciation are essential to assist the heart-centre to expand. Whenever we express thanks our energy field expands and lightens. An attitude of gratitude is very energetic and effective in manifesting whatever you may be wishing for.

It is simply about mindfulness; for every thought, word, action and deed we do there is a responsibility. By honouring ourselves we honour others. When we love ourselves unconditionally, we are able to love others in the same way. By offering heartfelt constructive criticism rather than being belittling, etc., then our auric field will shine brightly, even glow and expand.

Looking after our selves also means being aware of what we eat and drink. We are living proof of what we eat. When we eat healthy and drink plenty of water/fruit juices, we usually feel healthy and balanced. We experience great levels of vitality and well-being. If we eat too much junk food, then we feel sluggish and our vitality drops.

I often see patients who drink very little and are dehydrated. The body produces toxins through metabolism and a wide variety of bodily processes. Without fluid it has no means then of detoxifying itself, we may suffer with poor skin and sluggishness.

One patient I saw was full of toxicity; her fluid intake consisted of one cup of tea daily! Although she was a lovely person her aura was quite diminished, though still very light coloured, due to the fact that she had a lovely personality.

The reduction in size was simply due to the fact that her body was not able to flush away the natural by-products of digestion, metabolism, etc. Many women are infertile due simply to the fact that their wombs are dehydrated. The Australian Bush flower essence 'She Oak', rehydrates the womb and a very high percentage of women then become pregnant after taking the essence, usually within a months.

The Goldfish That Jumped

$e=mc^2$

Einstein wrote $e=mc^2$

E is energy in motion, just as we say E-MOTION.
Thus the more EMOTION we put into our lives
the more we attract whatever it is to us.

What I have learned is that there are what some call 'Spiritual Laws of The Universe' which apply to us as humans. By understanding them you can use them to your advantage – a bit like being in the flow rather than resisting. By understanding and appreciating these 'laws', you are able to plan your life to work with them rather than against them. This is how some people seem to be on 'easy street' whereas others are living in the school of hard knocks.

Which do you prefer? I know what I want, and I have had enough knocks thank you!

I have listed some here to help bring an understanding of how we create our own worlds. Over time, as we gain more understanding, we can learn to master our lives. Being mindful is essential because every thought, action, word and deed we do CREATES something. 'Mindful' simply means noticing or paying attention to what is going on in your head, and your response to the events going on around you.

The 'Law of attraction' is very simple. Basically, it says like attracts like, or birds of a feather flock together.

By becoming more aware of this, we begin to know where and who we should be around. If we are depressed, it is likely that we attract people around us who are also depressed. Likewise new mothers attract new mothers too.

So how can you now use this knowledge to help you in your everyday life?

For example, an artist seeking inspiration will most likely find it in art museum or in nature.

Like attracts like and having an understanding of energies and what thoughts we send daily to The Universe, we become more centred and balanced and more aware of all that we are capable of creating. Christ stated we have the power to move mountains. As humans we do, when we master mindfulness; that is, the art of choosing our thoughts, rather than our thoughts and emotions driving us.

How often have you said about someone, "He's always awkward". That person picks up the energy we have sent to them and, guess what, they are always awkward.

As the Dalai Lama once said - For whatever a man thinks about continually, to that his mind becomes inclined by force of habit.

Put another way: What we think about, we bring about. And the more passion and desire and enthusiastic action we take, the faster we bring it about.

We humans are energy beings. You and I are made up of energy, right down to the last atom and molecule.

$E=mc2$ – in simple words says: energy = mass x a big number.

In other words mass is made up of energy, which means that everything you can see, touch or feel is made up of energy, including animals, plants, trees, and rocks!

The Goldfish That Jumped

Did you know you receive and transmit energy continuously?

You create energy all the time, every time you eat something, your body changes food into energy. Every time you think something, your brain gives off energy, which some people can even pick up in the form of telepathy!

The Law of Attraction is a spiritual law which means, whatever thoughts we put out to The Universe, from our energy field, will be manifested. The more energy we put into them the quicker they will manifest.

However this is not an instant process. Sometimes things manifest in your life, years after you may have wanted them to!

People often say "Life is so hard, life is tough" and this is what they believe so this is what they manifest. This is why the rich get richer and the poor get poorer, because it is what they THINK that makes the difference, and where they put their focus and energy.

By recognizing and becoming more mindful and BEING PRESENT in the moment we can change our lives. This is why the present is called the present, because it is a PRESENT from the Universe.

The Buddhists might say that by becoming more aware of how you have created your life up to right now, the more aware of how you are creating right now, you become. And the good news is that if you created your current life, that means that you can change it to be however you wish, simply by changing your thinking!

So if you can change your mind-set; becoming more humanitarian, less critical and less judgmental of others, you become less critical of yourself. A quote by Zen Master Dogen explains this clearly: *"To study the way is to study the self; to study the self is to forget the self, to forget the self is to be enlightened by all things"*.

When we finally become aware of conditioned patterns of behaviour, and old expired habits, we can make a conscious choice to let them go. Although being on the Spiritual, Soulful path can be difficult and trying at times, overall those who are willing to "Walk the Walk" rather than just "Talk the Talk" and really embrace their own shortcomings and imperfections, benefit greatly.

That which we resist, we will eventually accept. So, we may resist our life lessons and our vulnerabilities. Yet, when we embrace them, we accept them as part of our being. We are what we are; good, bad and indifferent, and, rather than fighting this, if we accept who, and what we are, the world becomes a better place.

The less we judge ourselves, the less we are likely to judge others. We have all done things of which we are not proud. Things we often feel guilty about, hurtful things we may have said in an argument. By going within and looking at our shadow side: by being honest and really BEING IN THAT PAIN; then we can move on, accept and let it go. Letting go of our emotional baggage is an amazing feeling very, very liberating too.

"Let go and let God" is one of my friend's greatest sayings. By accepting and loving ourselves, we in turn accept others. Our energy field will reflect our true essence and our true nature and power. We begin to recognise that we are ALL ONE........ we ALL affect one another and we are each responsible for our thoughts, words, actions and deeds. This is also known as the "Law of Karma". If we do a good deed we accrue positive karma and vice versa.

Sometimes in order to experience and master a life lesson, we sign Karmic Contracts. Having had many Buddhist lifetimes, I had signed contracts in my past lives of experiencing only poverty. For this reason it was difficult, initially at least, for me to experience and welcome abundance into my life.

The Goldfish That Jumped

We sever Karmic Contracts by requesting The Lords of Karma to work with us and accept our wish to be free of the contracts which no longer serve us. This is often done through prayer and/or meditation.

I had always felt that if I had great wealth, it would affect who I am. I might become a rich bitch; rather like the character Goldie Hawn plays in "Overboard" (which just so happens to be my favourite film). I now see that this assumption was ridiculous. However, in previous lifetimes, having abundance MAY have distracted me from my life of discipline and learning.

Life lessons can be in trust, which we usually learn through mistrust. To experience love, we learn through having a broken heart. To be wholehearted, usually we have to be broken hearted. Tolerance is learnt through patience.

Usually we can recognize our life's lessons as they are often instances that keep repeating themselves or things in life which we really resist. Often people say, "I'd never do that" referring to someone else's behaviour, then, maybe in years to come, we display that behaviour. This is why it is always best not to judge.

If we can recognise and lose the urge to judge others, we eventually realize that we too are capable of misgivings. We are capable of being nasty and vindictive at times – so, therefore, why criticise it in others. If we stop criticising others, we in turn, will no longer attract critical people into our lives. The reason being that we have mastered this life lesson, we have understood that we created this in the first instance.

We then move closer to our soul and receive other life lessons. Healers will refer to this as "healing and peeling the layers, just like the layers of an onion." As we clear and unpeel one onion, we then begin on another one!

The Goldfish That Jumped

Moving On

*"Faith is the bird that feels the light when the
dawn is still dark".*

Rabindranath Tagore

Challenges and hurdles of various sizes will present themselves along the way and we do stumble from time to time. Anything that is worth having in life is worth that challenge – to me anyway. Whilst on this journey, I have had many times of doubt and then times of JOY.

Duality is another spiritual law. Male and female, black and white, Yin and Yang – the understanding and power of opposites. We need night to be able to enjoy daytime. Both are essential. We need to experience times of upset to welcome times of joy; otherwise how would we ever know one from the other. When we awaken from our deep sleep, we can then recognise how marvellous The Universe is in all its wonder.

Being spiritual doesn't have to mean that we wear hippie clothing, numerous crystals necklaces, bracelets, having spiky hair and/or pointed shoes. We do not need to advertise we are spiritual. We certainly can do those things............ we find what is right for us and LEARN TO BE. We start to live in harmony and go with the flow, accepting all is as it should be.

I had constantly thought of life as "hard" and full of "doom and gloom". So, I'd created a hard life, full of doom and gloom. My own shortcomings had brought these things to me. What a very powerful and VERY PAINFUL REALIZATION. I had been the one who had manifested a very messy divorce, a lack of finances, lack of support in relationships and all the other aspects of my life that had been difficult and extremely challenging.

I had lived my life full or fear, doubt, guilt and worry – the four worst energies we can hold. These negative energies are so dense they make us feel like as are carrying the world on our shoulders. My body was heavy and tired, holding onto these thoughts and heavy feelings. I'd manifested a life in an ever spinning circle to keep fuelling fear, doubt and worry. WHAT A REVELATION. It smacked hard. I began to visualize abundance and love in my life……….. and, with this new understanding, my life began to change.

Be Careful What You Wish For

"Undoubtedly, we become what we envisage"
Claude M. Bristol

I began to live more wholeheartedly and wholesomely too. Every morning, I would start my day by asking for help from The Divine. Then, I would be open and listen. I would look diligently for coincidences, or synchronous events, that would possibly affect my destiny, and, wherever relevant, would act on that guidance.

So, for example, we might ask for guidance relating to a possible career move. A friend may then call and inform us of a job they have seen advertised, then we listen to the radio and the same job is advertised. If we still haven't recognised what the Universe is trying to tell us, a third example will manifest; we buy a newspaper and the job we want is advertised, we open it at exactly the right page. It is essential that we recognise these coincidences, and, if it feels right, act upon them.

If I followed The Law of Attraction, this was possible, as was everything else. I welcomed in positive people, positive situations and daily I became more and more positive. As my awareness of my past lives deepened, so I attracted in people who were also very aware of their past lives too. In fact, more recently a friend asked if I would work with him. "We've done it before, in past lives, so why not do it again?" he asked.

My soul began to open and flower. (This is why I have a rose on my business logo). It was like a whole new world was appearing before me. It had been there all along – only now I could feel it, see it and taste it. Now I had to learn to live it and BE AT ONE WITH IT.

My search continued. I read "The Atlantis Blueprint" as déjà vu of Atlantis began to gather strength. Often clients, through their readings, brought yet another piece to my ever growing jigsaw. Frequently, upon first meeting me, they would greet me and say "I know you, don't I?" It was always established that we had not meet previously, despite the obvious familiarity and knowing between us. By now déjà vu had become an accepted part of everyday life.

In November 2002 I attended an Angel workshop with Tina. She introduced me to Marianne. We got on famously, feeling like we had known one another for a lifetime. The bond was instant and magical. I am very grateful, and always will be, to this wonderful friend, who, I was soon to realize, changed my life for the better. There is a Buddhist saying;

"When the student is ready, the Master will appear – the student will then teach the Master".

Fast Track Learning

"As the bee takes the essence of a flower and
flies away without destroying its beauty and perfume,
so let the sage wander in this life"

Dalai Lama

My Master had appeared. Thank you. Marianne and I spent the day together laughing and joking, enjoying the workshop. Part of the day, which was particularly special, was when I met a lady who had a rose quartz crystal skull. She knew me, without having met me previously, that knowing intuition meant that she knew it was appropriate for me to hold the skull. What an experience and a privilege.

Crystals hold energy; a small quartz crystal will charge a battery for a very long time. The skulls hold information, just like a computer memory board. Information relating to The Akashic Records, how man came to exist and a wide range of other spiritual teachings were held in this skull. Many pictures flashed in my minds' eye. It was a miracle. Some I recognized and some I did not at the time.

For me as a psychic; I get pictures and a sense of knowing whenever I hold a person's hand or I hold stones in a stone circle or a crystal skull. Some of the pictures related back to Atlantis, an ancient civilisation of times gone by. I had recently begun to experience déjà vu of Atlantis, much was confirmed when I held the skull. In fact, when its owner met me she stated that she had known me from Atlantis.

By now I was much more accepting of my past lives, my knowing and my inner wisdom. Although the initial déjà vu had shocked me, this was a total acceptance of all that is. Marianne was meant to be there, Betty was meant to have the skull with her, she was meant to recognize and meet me, and I was certainly meant to meet them both.

The original crystal skulls were created by the extra-terrestrials. They are exact replicas of the human skull with incredible detail of the eye sockets, teeth, nose etc. They are life-size skulls made of crystal. Some are made of clear quartz, others smoky quartz, lapis lazuli, amethyst, etc.

There are 13 in the world and they have been studied by top scientists over the years. In recent times, the company Hewlett Packard tried to replicate a skull with the most up to date laser technology. Each time the crystal shattered, they concluded that science cannot comprehend how they were created initially.

We had all thoroughly enjoyed the workshop and Marianne and I agreed to keep in touch. The bond was huge and wonderful too. She willingly agreed to teach me Reiki as soon as possible. The Universe had other ideas............

A Little Diversion

*"It's very helpful to realize that the emotions we have,
the negativity and the positivity, are exactly what we need
to be fully human, fully awake, fully alive."*

Pema Chodron

My head was in a spin and I felt like everything was coming at me at once. I now know my journey was accelerating fast, but back then all I knew, was that I was scared and I felt like my life was changing rapidly. Maybe the changes were so rapid, that I might get left behind.

In December 2002, I contracted gastro-enteritis, a simple tummy upset, or so I thought. I became seriously ill and spent many an unhappy hour with my head down the toilet. This went on for days and days.

Little did I know at the time, how my life was about to be thrown into turmoil, and how I would be forced to walk the path of the soul with a life lesson in TRUST. TRUST that The Universe would take care of me financially, and that, eventually I would indeed, return to health. I was very physically fit and healthy, prior to the gastro-enteritis, so, it seemed very odd to me, that, after two weeks I struggled to stand up and dress myself.

I felt as weak as a kitten, and often my head was full of dark thoughts, 'what if this doesn't go away? What if I can't look after the children?' My mum was already coming over every day, for how much longer could she cope. I was a serious burden

119

on everyone, and I kept on trying to be strong for them, and each time, my illness got the better of me, and had to lie down to recover myself for long periods.

This was shocking to me. I had always been a "get up and go" person. Normally I would quickly bounce back to health. Now I was shattered, constantly. What on earth could be causing all this? I began to wonder what it might be? This was becoming serious.

Everything was an effort – getting up in the morning with the children, making their breakfasts, washing up and putting out the washing. It was a most painful time because as the weeks went on, I felt useless.

Having been very physically fit throughout my life prior to my illness; such as easily hiking 10 miles without any problems, I was astonished to be unable to walk across a room without a huge effort. I began to have much greater respect for the sick and the old who manage to make normal lives despite their difficulties.

Life began to feel very unfair. Now walking 100 yards would exhaust me. I had to carefully plan my day. My mother was a Godsend and used to take me shopping because the drive itself would tire me out – never mind wandering endless aisles of the supermarket. It's funny how, even now, I can still recall the extreme tiredness and feeling so helpless. Having to care for four children was hard enough, now I was barely able to care for myself.

I was heartbroken and bewildered. I had only had a tummy upset and life had never been the same. The weeks turned into months and I was becoming increasingly scared that I would be like this forever. I missed walking, I missed my freedom to just get up and drive in the car.

Now my world had been turned on its head. Everything had to be planned; I had to establish and estimate how much energy

I had in the morning, then make a decision as to which jobs needed to be done, and, which could wait. If I did too much, I would be even more tired than normal. I quickly learnt that overdoing things could mean that I would be completely out of action for two whole days.

Eventually I began to feel dispirited and disheartened. I seemed to have come so far and now............ well, I was going nowhere fast. Marianne was such a life-saver, I telephoned her most days and she was always patient with me. She recognized I was heading towards depression and that in itself began to frighten me. It would have been so easy to turn to the doctor and request antidepressants. To this day I thank her for preserving my sanity.

Regular trips to the doctors for sick notes would physically exhaust me. I found it so hard not to fall asleep in the waiting room, especially if I had to wait more than twenty minutes. The frustration mounted. After three months of having to manage what precious energy I had, another trip to the doctors was now part of my routine.

I arrived on time and was aware that this time I was due to see a new GP. She was lovely, but, being unfamiliar with my case asked me to trawl through EVERYTHING. I was very close to tears.

"I only had gastro-enteritis" I blurted, "Oh, but your notes here state that you were very unwell. Gastro-enteritis kills people every year; not just the elderly, but young people in their thirties..... like YOU. You could have easily died of that." I was speechless.

"You seem very angry" she said. "Yes, I suppose I am. I used to be SO busy, now I feel useless." My frustration was mounting by the second.

"I think you have Chronic Fatigue Syndrome" she casually suggested. "You'll be like this forever, so, you may as well get rid of your hiking boots because you won't be hiking ever again. Get used to the idea and get used to living life in this way. I will contact the hospital. They will contact YOU for an appointment with the specialist. I will sign you off for two months and await the consultant's report. "

Just like that, in her matter of fact way, I had been slapped down, told to give up and felt as though I had been binned!!! The penny dropped in my head with a massive clunk. I was gob-smacked. I had studied biology and had many friends in the NHS. I had always had an interest in medicine. I had the classic symptoms. It had been staring me in the face but, I guess I had not wanted to see it.

I felt so incredibly sad. I was absolutely heartbroken. I had come so far on my journey and now this!!!

I arrived home, shocked and completely heartbroken. I felt the full weight of hopelessness and despair. I was deeply upset, beyond any measure of upset I had ever experienced before. Where am I to go now? What is my life going to be like? Is this the end for me?

In my grief-stricken state, I telephoned my dad. At the same time I cried bitter, heartfelt tears. "Don't tell mum, they have told me that I will never walk again. I will dad; just you wait and see……."

That day I cried what seemed endless tears of anger, frustration and injustice. I was a hardworking woman. Why had this happened to me? I vowed then, that I would do everything in my power to get well. EVERYTHING.

The hospital appointment card duly arrived. This meant another day of managing my ever reducing energies. As the hospital car park was huge, it meant I had to ensure I slept for at least an hour before I set off. Otherwise, it would be most likely that I could fall asleep. A very busy hospital and the probability of a long wait were not really appealing to me.

The Goldfish That Jumped

When I eventually saw the consultant, he agreed with what the doctor had mentioned in the referral letter. The consultation was short and to the point. "We diagnose after six months, so I will see you again then."

That was it, no emotion, no advice, no support, nothing. I felt like a cow in a cattle market, another wheel in a machine. There had been no emotions in his words and not even a smile. Rightly or wrongly, by now, I had come to expect this behaviour; so, I left the hospital exhausted, again, hopeless and no wiser.

I'd been too exhausted to work for months, too tired to manage to attend T'ai Chi and my only solace was reading books. I recall my very dear friend Julie, telling me that the illness allowed every cell in my body to transform into light. I understand it now but, at the time, I certainly did not. Day by day, long and painful, unproductive as they were, with the help of my children, my family and my dear friend Marianne, I just about managed to hold my soul together.

The Goldfish That Jumped

A Little Light of Hope at the End of the Tunnel

"In the middle of difficulty lies opportunity"

Albert Einstein

Marianne helped me to keep my hopelessness and feelings of despair at bay. There were times where they could consume me, rather like a tsunami. When I had first become ill she had attuned me to Reiki One; in the hope that it would help me to recover. Now, faced with the possibility of a life-sentence with this illness, she recommended she attune me in Reiki Two. I duly agreed and we set a date.

The 26th June 2003 was to be a special day, a day I will always remember. I learnt about absent healing and it was a delight to spend the day with her. She is a very gifted teacher and an incredibly powerful healer too. Having done the Reiki Two course, she suggested I consider my Masters. We agreed and, within two weeks I was attuned as a Reiki Master. This meant that I could now teach. My energy and zest for life were finally returning. Life turned around swiftly and wonderfully.

At around the same time, my dear friend Sophie was studying Homeopathy and was looking for "guinea pigs". I agreed as I had nothing to lose and, anyway, that's the sort of thing I do.........
agree to help people, even if it means being a "Guinea pig". We had met through T'ai Chi – again, another valued friend. One with whom I felt very familiar and comfortable with instantly. Homeopathy is often referred to as T.E.E.T.H. tried everything else, now try Homeopathy!

The Goldfish That Jumped

At this time, my manager in the Civil Service was under pressure from his bosses to establish whether or not I would be returning to work. It is such a huge organisation, my individuality and soulfulness, could not be sustained in this environment.

The job I had once enjoyed, I had now outgrown. It was time to move on. There was NO contest. I knew in my soul I could NEVER return to a job without job satisfaction and fulfilment. I told him honestly that I doubted my return. I explained what both the doctor and specialist had said and knew I had to severe that cord.

I hoped that, once well again, my business would succeed. That I would be able to support myself and my children, pay my bills easily and finally embrace my life, have some control and LIVE…. THE GOLDFISH WAS READY TO JUMP.

A Lesson in Trusting Myself

*"Every man takes the limits of his own field of vision,
for the limits of the world."*

Arthur Schopenhauer

The initial Homeopathy consultation was very detailed; the consultation was so unlike anything I had experienced at the doctors, or the hospital. I was treated with respect, individuality and asked a multitude of questions. What was my childhood like? How had I felt after the divorce? How had I managed with the children? What were the children like?

Details of previous illnesses I had had were listed in her notes and it was incredibly revealing. As I told my life story, I realised my whole life had been a struggle. It was a very painful experience, though most enlightening. No wonder I had been ill and had been forced to rest by The Universe. She was patient, kind and understanding, especially when I BEGAN TO CRY.

I became aware that the illness was a mirror of my internal anger and my frustrations at never doing what I wanted to do which was to study and train in medicine and TO BE LOVED. This had, in fact, been a manifestation of all those years of not taking care of myself. It was all related to the times when I had abandoned my Inner light, and misunderstood the preciousness of my soul.

This was to become very instrumental in inspiring me to study Homeopathy and, later, to become a Homeopath. Though I was very sad at the end of the consultation, I recognized at a much deeper level, that I had the absolute power to change. I recognised that, despite the difficulties in my life, I had a deep and unique strength that was a very powerful realisation indeed.

It was nothing short of a miracle that I had, after all, got to this point in my life. Now that I was aware of who I was, what had shaped me, how I was, and how I had already started the process of change, I was becoming aware that I could take back my power, power in making even more changes for a brighter, better future. I took my remedy bottle of Phosphorous and the journey to recovery commenced.

OUR FULL HEALTH ALLOWS US TO BE THE COMPLETE AND HEALTHY SOUL THAT WE WERE MEANT TO BE. DIS-EASE IS JUST AN ENERGETIC IMBALANCE.

As I gathered my strength and stamina, I knew that I was now ready to start a new relationship. This time it would be with a clear realisation on my part, that I deserved better than I had had previously in a relationship. I had grown up in my own emotional and spiritual maturity and had to honour that deeper level of learning and understanding.

Having been alone now, for almost two years, I didn't really know where to begin to look for a new friend/partner. I do not normally buy a newspaper but, as there are no coincidences in The Universe, this particular day I bought the local rag. I looked in the "Singles" section.

There was a man who seemed okay with the brief description that was listed and I decided to phone him. We agreed to meet in a local public house. I looked at his aura, which was a little dim and grey and knew that I no longer wanted someone who had unresolved emotional problems. I needed a fresh start, a new beginning. However, I was happy to chat for the evening, although I promised myself that was that.

We chatted and I explained my work as a psychic reader and a healer. He was both curious and interested, in the fact that I had always seen and heard things, which most other people do not experience. He was also curious about my work as a healer. As we chatted he stated that his ex-partner was very interested in this field and suggested I phone her. I hadn't met this lady, neither had I known anything about her.

Trusting my intuition, I knew I had to telephone her. She answered the phone and we just clicked immediately. She explained that she worked in a massage therapy centre locally, and, went on to explain that she, and her friend Clara, worked together. She passed on Clara's number, as she owned the business.

Again, I followed my intuition and knew I had to telephone this woman. When I spoke to her, her voice seemed familiar and through the conversation the feeling of knowing grew deeper. Then, without any hesitation, she agreed that I could start working in her clinic with immediate effect. She hadn't even met me, but explained that she was merely comfortable with her gut instinct and that was enough confirmation to her, that it was the right decision.

I explained to her that I would like to look around the premises firstly. We agreed to meet at the therapy centre the following day. Upon seeing her I recognised her face, she then in turn recognised me too. We had attended the same school, although she was slightly older than me. We soon established that I had been in the same year, at school, as her younger brother. I started work within the week. They had a wonderful trust with their clientele and recommended my services immediately. I had numerous clients within a very short time indeed.

The combination of the Homeopathy and the Reiki worked. Within a month I ran a clinic in Longridge and LOVED my work. No longer was "work" a four letter word ending with "K". One of my first patients, all those years ago, when I worked in the clinic, was a lady who would soon become one of my favourite clients. As she walked in I noticed her energy field was very dim and very tired-looking. Elizabeth was terminally ill and I knew.

In these situations the ethics are huge; what a dilemma. I needed to know if she was aware of her own failing physical health. I had begun to send healing, even before I shook her hand and welcomed her into my consulting room. Holding her space very lovingly, I gently asked her name and address, then mentioned that she did not appear to be "firing on all six"…….. "No" she replied.

I needed more information because I certainly would have suggested she see a doctor. Despite knowing her physical energies were low, I knew she was a wholesome, loving lady. I knew she had a beautiful personality, and I continued, whilst sending more magic healing and holding her space very respectfully. "Your energy seems a little low" I stated very, very gently. She burst into tears and blurted out that she had terminal cancer and had been given three months to live.

She was relieved to know, that I knew how seriously ill she was. She cried for most of the session and I encouraged her to do that, as I do with all my patients and clients. As I listened, I continued to send her healing throughout the session. Finally, when we had finished the healing, she said she felt much better after the treatment. Her daughter had suggested that she meet me, as she herself was trained as a Reiki healer. Her daughter and I met several months later and we are still good friends.

Elizabeth became a regular client, and, I have to say a respected and dear friend. She survived for well over three months, I am almost sure it was approximately eighteen. We were in touch frequently. Inevitably, there came a time when her health deteriorated so much that I had grown concerned. I had a deep and painful knowing, that things were not right.

We all have to die at some point, but healing in any form is a miracle, it can help the person pass over peacefully. Within 24 hours of my knowing and nagging feelings, her daughter had telephoned me. She explained that her mother had recently received chemotherapy and was indeed, very poorly. My worst fears were confirmed. A home visit was suggested, as she was far too weak and ill to travel.

Despite wanting to cry, I remained professional and provided a beautiful healing treatment for her. I knew this would be the last time I would ever see her alive. I sent healing daily after that visit and she died several days later. I still miss her to this day and, over the years have felt her presence close to me. Even as I write this part of the book she is stood to my right.

I met many new and inspirational people. People from all walks of life, from top business people to domestic goddesses: becoming good friends with many of them. I respected my body and worked a reasonable number of hours in the clinic without overdoing things. This was something which I had never done before. My strength grew, although I had not dared push too hard, and certainly hadn't dared to hike, or even consider hiking. Then, in September of 2003........ I met George.

The Goldfish That Jumped

New Lessons

"Love is a temporary madness, it erupts like a volcano and then subsides. And when it subsides you have to make a decision. You have to work out whether your roots have so entwined together that it is inconceivable that you should ever part. Love itself is what is left over when being in love has burned away, and this is both an art and a fortunate accident .... we had it, we had roots that grew towards each other underground, and when all the pretty blossom had fallen from our branches we found that we were one tree and not two. But sometimes the petals fall away and the roots have not entwined"

Louis de Bernieres -
An extract from Captain Corelli's Mandolin

George's name "jumped out at me" from my diary. I felt I knew this man and though I was only due to meet him in two weeks time, I felt a link on some level. That day, he was my final appointment and was booked in for a reading and a healing. Upon meeting him, I knew I knew him.

He was not very spiritual and was quite unaware at the time. I usually do the reading first, then the healing. In this way, the client can talk to me and ask any questions. He seemed happy with that and I duly started the reading. The pictures flooded in to my third eye, so clear and so amazing too.

I "saw" his businesses, his family and home, I then "saw" myself in the reading, a villa in Samos, Greece and our relationship!!! I explained to him what I saw, and, that I could see a new love. He asked me what she looked like. As you can imagine, I was rather shocked at seeing myself in these pictures/ visions. In my haste, I answered "Penelope Cruz!"

The scenario is funny now, when I look back. What a dilemma to be in. Back then, I just couldn't think of anything else to say. I certainly look nothing like Miss Cruz. Anyways, he seemed happy with that and the reading continued. All the points raised in the reading were confirmed, he was delighted.

Following the reading, I commenced the healing, which usually takes about an hour. His heart centre was so damaged, there was very little energy. It took me over 90 minutes to reactivate the heart centre chakra.

In energy medicine, we are trained to re-balance, and re-energize various parts of the body. The heart centre is one of the most important centres. When balanced, the heart centre will allow us to connect with our Higher Self, our Soul. It allows us to give and receive love and to be open- hearted.

His energy was almost non-existent. I was quite concerned and spent almost an hour on his heart centre alone. (When energy gets stuck, or becomes stagnant; especially in the heart area, it is often likely that the person will suffer heart pathology. It is usually a good indication of probable heart attack, angina, etc.). I was still very concerned for his well-being when he left.

Several appointments later he asked if I would like to go walking with him. I was delighted to be asked and had looked forward to this day for over a week. I felt like a child who was in the biggest sweet shop. Our first hike was approximately seven miles long. This was my first serious walk in almost a year. The joy of putting on my hiking boots was something in itself.

Being back in the open countryside was an amazing experience for me; breath-taking and very emotional for several reasons. I was with a man I was very fond of; actually I was in love with him. At this time though, I was keeping my feelings very much to myself. I was able to walk again in my beloved countryside.

The Goldfish That Jumped

My life was coming together and I had a career that I loved. During the walk, apart from being slightly out of breath whilst walking uphill, I had no aches, no pains, and NO tiredness. It was a miracle. I'd done it, I had achieved my quest to hike again and here I was, enjoying every single, blissful moment.

Just as we were about to get in the car at the end of the walk, George explained how he felt about me. Our relationship began. I had loved my first husband, the children's father, very deeply. We had been together for over ten years, but I loved this man more than I had ever loved anyone before. It was very overwhelming and beautiful.

That night, after he had dropped me off at home, I clearly remember phoning my friend Pauline. I was crying and sobbing whilst on the phone. "What is the matter?" she asked......... "You're crying so much, are you okay? Has someone died?" "Oh no" I replied, "I have met someone and he has the capability, with the power of this love, to destroy me. I love him so much I have to walk this road." "Well, enjoy the ride" she replied and laughed."

Little did I know then how true my words were to become. Our relationships teach us our most valued lessons in life. Mine was about to become a journey many varied and colourful. .... and one that very nearly destroyed me.

Our relationship happened very fast. Initially people accused us of having an affair, thinking we had been together for months, if not years. We were inseparable, sharing everything and delighted to be in one another's company. Soon, we were not just looking for a home together in Britain, but also abroad, in Greece. Each day was a joy and I loved being with him.

I now understand that when we have had past lives together as friends/lovers/brothers or sisters we automatically re-join at the point where we previously left off. George and I had had a wonderful loving marriage before, so therefore, we merely re-joined at that point again.

The Goldfish That Jumped

Deja Vu

"Our whole business therefore in this life, is to restore to health the eye of the heart whereby God may be seen"

Saint Augustine

At around about the age of ten, I recall a "picture" in my mind's eye, which I had, come to understand would be representative my future. I was outside a huge house, the drive was curved at the front and I was stood with our four children; three sons and a daughter. I was with a partner, I assumed him to be my husband.

Even at that tender age, I became aware that my worst fear would be that I would be widowed, to lose my beloved partner. These were very powerful emotions and I felt them – even at that young age. I also knew at this early age that I needed to visit Greece.

Greece always held a particular magic for me, the mythology and the love stories of the Gods. The Grecian artefacts, the whole culture fascinated me. I loved watching any documentaries relating to Greek civilizations. I loved reading about Greece and any stories pertaining to this marvellous country.

I knew at some stage I would visit, and, I really hoped, as a child, that I would get an opportunity as soon as I was old enough to travel alone. I hoped it would be the first place I would visit abroad.

Looking back to the time we spent in Greece, we had a friend who taught me basic Greek. Her mother often sat with us and she spoke no English. As I learnt the pronunciations, her mother would often interrupt, stating that I had visited Greece before and was pretending that I was learning the language, that I already knew Greek!!!

She was astounded that I could pronounce even the most difficult words. I am a quick learner I admit, but certainly hadn't ever spoken Greek before. Yet, it did seem easy and familiar.

Obviously I had lived here in my past lives, by this stage in my soul's journey I had a deepened knowing, and acceptance of this fact. I am not a sun-worshipper and try to stay out of it, whenever possible. Yet, within 24 hours I was so tanned I looked Greek!

I recall one morning, as I walked into the village for bread, passing some tourists and greeting them cheerily with "Kalimeera" (Good morning), the man replied "Good morning" with an unmistakeable English accent. Even the English people thought I was Greek!!!

Often, when I greeted the locals, they too would think I was Greek, and would often reply to a simple greeting by answering with a full conversation .... which would leave me wondering whether or not I would ever get to grips with this language!!!

Greek is said to be the most difficult language to learn, other than Japanese. It is easier for the Greeks to learn English, rather than for the English to then learn Greek.

In the reading with George I had seen a house in Greece. It was very clear and very detailed. The house was situated on a bend in the road, detached, painted white and had a mountain to the rear. I could see the sea in the distance and the beautiful fig trees, together with row, upon row of grape vines. It was absolutely stunning.

The Goldfish That Jumped

George had visited Samos a year before we meet. My belief is that as we had had past lives there; teaching spirituality and providing healing to the community and surrounding islands, on some level, he was trying to rekindle that energy and ..... who knows, maybe he had been trying to find me.

We are often drawn to certain places and as each place has its own energy. By revisiting, we bring back and rekindle that energy, if pertinent, into our soul. It may provide us with inspiration and creative ideas. It may bring a profound peacefulness, one that we have never previously experienced.

If we remain open-hearted, we can experience the most powerful of connections on a soul to soul level. Samos had that magic about it and George wanted to buy a property out there, and, at that time, was hoping he would retire there too.

In the May of 2004 we arrived at Samos airport. It was the first time I had ever travelled abroad. With four children to support, having a limited budget meant that there were no opportunities for foreign travel. Besides, I felt it would be difficult to manage all four children. What if two of them were struggling in the swimming pool or I lost one of them in a crowded city or at the airport?

I can clearly recall walking down the aircraft steps and feeling the heat hitting my face. The sight of the mountains was marvellous and I had an immense feeling of coming home. Samos touched my soul instantly. I was overwhelmed and felt so connected to this magical place. We travelled to Pythagorio harbour and walked by the seafront.

Pythagorio is named after Pythagoras, the famous mathematician and philosopher. The water was so clear we could see the fish swimming. From the harbour, lay the coast of Turkey and the wonderful Turkish mountains. It all seemed so familiar, I felt so peaceful and content here.

It was all new to me and I felt like a little girl, experiencing the world through new eyes. We ate in a taverna situated on the harbour wall. The Greek waiter and the lovely accent, the music in the background, it was all truly magical. My first experience of Greece was wonderful.

Later that day we had arranged to meet with an estate agent, one whom George had liaised with frequently. The estate agent welcomed us to his office and to Greece. He was an extraordinary fellow; large stature, even bigger personality and smoked a pipe. His English was extremely good – just as well, because our Greek was extremely poor!!!

Soon we were travelling up and down dirt tracks, steep hillsides and up mountain trails viewing several properties. It was incredible and exciting too. We viewed the whole island, looking at houses near the coast, in mountain villages and some, which were so remote, I often wondered, if we lived there, if we would ever find our way home.

There were lots of stories attached to the houses; foreigners who purchased or built the property, then had to move on, families where the children had grown up and some based on politics! All those we viewed were unsuitable for a huge variety of reasons. Some were too small, access was poor and some were in terrible states of disrepair, without access for builders, and/or the materials they would require for renovation.

We couldn't find the home we wanted and decided that we would ask the locals in each village for their advice. One particular mountain village proved to be our favourite place. We agreed a house here would be perfect. The views were spectacular and amazing; it felt like home, and, best of all, it housed our favourite taverna too.

There were many local mountain walks, the access up to the village was reasonable. It was situated on the Northern side of the island, which meant there was an abundance of greenery, rather than the barren landscape of the south. It was also situated very close to our favourite town and beach, and, I almost forgot to mention, our favourite bakery; which was actually the most favoured on the whole island.

We knew we would eventually find somewhere we loved to live and we never lost heart. In fact, from the many houses we visited, we took ideas and inspiration. We enjoyed the scenery and the way the estate agent passed on information about the local people and folklore too. Our learning's were great and it was all an adventure.

Although much of our time was taken up looking for property, we thoroughly enjoyed our stay; the sea, scenery and the Greek cuisine. We were both sad to leave at the end of the week. We stayed in Kokkari and from there we often walked the footpath up the mountainside to our favourite village. Nothing in The Universe is coincidence.

George had a holiday booked to this wonderful island a month later. It had been booked twelve months previously, and, as it was for two weeks, I felt it inappropriate for me to leave the children for any longer than a week. We had quite a dilemma and eventually we agreed that he should go, alone. We had the rest of our lives to look forward to together; two weeks apart would be fine!

So, he left with his friends and we both spent two weeks missing one another. Although we spoke daily, I must admit, I was thoroughly miserable. I felt like a huge part of me was missing. It seems crazy looking back; I lost over a stone in that time, and was definitely love-sick.

Whilst out there walking from Kokkari, up to our favourite village, he came across an old house, derelict, and in quite a bad state of repair. It was on the outskirts of our favourite village and we had walked this footpath often. Why had we not seen it before? George being George, an eager and very capable businessman, was not about to let this opportunity slip him by. He called me and asked what he should do.

Without hesitation, I suggested he trust his judgement, my intuition was absolutely positive. "Go get it; if it feels right for you." I said. He made enquiries and notified the bank of his intentions. He signed the contracts to the property on the morning of his departure. Upon his return we agreed never to be parted again!!!

"Make plans and make God laugh" is something my dear friend Dennis often says. Little did we know what would be around the corner.

A New Home

"Life was never meant to be a struggle just a gentle progression from one point to another, much like walking through a valley on a sunny day."

Stuart Wilde

As work on the house, in the beautiful Greek mountain village got underway, we continued to look for a home in England. We travelled all over Lancashire and were frequently disappointed.

One November morning, we set off just before eight, to travel the suburbs of Preston. We travelled up and down the area, some areas which neither of us had ever visited before. Three quarters of a mile down one particular country lane – just as we were about to turn back, we spotted an old farmhouse, derelict, neglected and desperately in need of tender, loving care.

It seemed too good to be true. After months of searching fruitlessly, could this really become our dream house? We immediately stopped the car, right in the middle of the road. It was lucky no-one was about. We promptly parked up and looked at the huge farmhouse, neglected and seemingly unloved. We were both very excited to take a closer look and to find out more.

The garden was so overgrown and full of weeds that it was difficult to manoeuvre, in order to get right up to the house. As we peered in through the algae covered windows, we were very pleased at what we saw. At the back of the house an external door was open and we peered in. The house was in such a poor state of repair, we were under no illusions that it was going to be easy to undertake such a massive project.

As we stood back from the house, we could both visualise it finished and standing in its glorious self. We were both thrilled. It was far too early to phone the estate agent to arrange a viewing. I had clients booked in the clinic that morning, and I was very tempted to cancel, in order that I could go with George to view the house.

Once I had finished with my clients I telephoned him to establish whether or not he had arranged a viewing. He told me he had put in an offer for the property. We were delighted; at last we had found somewhere we could live.

New Beginnings

From a tiny acorn, huge oak tree forests grow!

We were both so excited at the prospect of a new home and a new beginning. After waiting for what seemed like years, at last, the end was in sight. The house had been so neglected and was desperately in need of very tender, loving care. We were eager to get started, as we knew this would further cement our relationship, whilst also deepening our commitment to one another.

Both George and I are forward thinkers and like to plan effectively. We would often be heard saying the Six P Principle: Proper planning prevents pretty poor performance. This house restoration was to be a mammoth task. The house was derelict and uninhabitable. It was without a kitchen or bathrooms, although it did have running water.

Finding bathroom suites and a kitchen, to match the history of the place would be a challenge. Ensuring the designs were in keeping with the property and its authenticity, presented a very real problem. However, in my usual fashion I asked The Universe for help and we sourced wonderful showrooms, for both bathroom and kitchen.

From the beginning of the project, we both decided that it would be lovely to restore the house to its former glory. This would mean that we would keep as many of the original features as possible, restoring them to their optimum, and, also to be extremely selective as we knew many new fixtures and fittings would be required. They would have to be designed to match the original decor.

Originally built in 1700, the house was over 300 years old. It was a detached farmhouse, built from hand-made red bricks and stood empty and lonely. It had seventeen rooms in total. The house was designed in an 'L' shape. From the entrance hallway, the doorway led off to the right to two living rooms. To the left, was the rest of the house, another lounge, utility room, what would soon become the kitchen and the magnificent wooden staircase.

Upstairs lay another four bedrooms and three bathrooms, then a further staircase leading to the attic space. Many of the floorboards were rotten and in fact, the estate agents' manageress had recently broken her ankle here, whilst she was showing previous prospective buyers around the property. Little did I know at the time, that she was later to become a very dear and valued friend.

It had been empty for many years and over that time, woodworm had caused much damage to the beams, floorboards, etc. In fact, the woodwork throughout the house had been affected and would need treating. Most of the few remaining doors were made of oak and had the original latches on them. The others would need to be replaced completely.

The extent of the task was huge, yet, we were both dedicated and, despite knowing the extent of the restoration work, we never doubted that we could achieve that, which we set out to do. We never faltered or wavered in our passion, nor our determination.

Being such an old property, full of heritage and rare features, it was a Grade Two listed building. This meant that planning permission would be required, before any structural work could begin. This we knew would delay our plans by up to two months. Thus, as the earliest opportunity George contacted them for their approval and advice.

Many centuries ago there was a tax called "window tax". The more windows a property had, the more the owners paid to the government. Therefore, many large houses, obviously with many windows in their properties, would be bricked up, in order to reduce costs. It was clear by looking at the external walls, that there were different types of bricks; indicating that many of the windows had been closed.

By restoring the house to its former glory, these would have to be re-opened, new frames constructed and the building regulations followed accurately. In such an old property, double glazing was certainly not an option.

The plans were discussed with the building inspector; besides the replacement windows, permission was required to rebuild some of the external walls, as they had more lumps and bumps than Blackpool pleasure beach!!!

Initially, whilst waiting for the go-ahead from the local council, we knocked off the perished plaster and spent many hours researching and sourcing materials. We engaged a local building merchants company to gather information about new window frames, door frames, etc., as these would all have to be built to the original specifications; those of many centuries ago.

Many specialists were called in for estimates and their opinions welcomed. Each of them was in awe of the massive task that we had undertaken. Most mentioned they doubted we would ever finish, though said they would admire us, if we did ever manage to complete the full restoration of this huge property. Not once, did we ourselves doubt that this would indeed become our home.

I even recall going to work on the house, being covered in dust and sweat, whilst I had a bout of influenza and, though I felt very ill, I was delighted to be involved in this restoration, a joint and lovely adventure for the two of us.

The population generally then, were much shorter in stature than people of today. This meant that beams and door frames were lower than those today. This also created problems and many head injuries too!

Each and every day progress could be seen. We were filled with enthusiasm and remained focused on our goal. My sons helped and loved meeting the various workmen. Many of those friendships still remain today. We all have precious memories and the camaraderie was wonderful, too.

Eventually, in February the following year, permission was granted to demolish the gable end wall and rebuild in hand-made bricks which we had scoured from a local reclamation yard. As soon as we got the news, we telephoned the builders who were on site. It was ten o'clock in the morning. We visited the house at lunch time and were amazed to find that the wall was already demolished! Our enthusiasm had over spilled to our team too.

Piece by piece we managed to restore the farmhouse. A local wood turner amazed us by producing spindles to replace those affected by woodworm. A friend suggested we leave the hallway free of plaster, and place spotlights at certain points, so that the brickwork would add an additional feature of authenticity to the place. Once the chimneys were re-pointed, the fireplaces restored, new plaster and door frames were fitted; the end was finally in sight.

We were both looking forward to moving in to our dream home.

Or so it would be in a perfect world...... but The Universe was about to spin the goldfish bowl in an unexpected direction.

Illusions

"Life is an illusion so choose a good one"
Christine Comaford

Bizarre though it can be to realise, the old mystics say 'Life is an illusion', one way to understand this to realise that we each assume that others' perceptions of the world are the same as our own, even though there are huge amounts of evidence to the contrary!

We all make assumptions in life, many on a daily basis. I had always seen energy fields and this was so natural to me that it never crossed my mind that others did not see them. Around this time George was looking for a new artist in his business. He asked if I would sit in whilst he conducted interviews for the position.

One particular lady had a very large light, bright aura. It was very clear, without dirt or any markings. This was significant of her clear emotional state, well-being and spiritual connection to Source.

She was intelligent and an excellent communicator, without ego, and as such, would be an excellent team player, her light shone like a beacon. Her intuition was sharp; this too, assisting her in her work as an artist. The physical health was at a peak so, all in all, she was perfect for the job.

Following the interview, I recall him asking me at the end of the interview what I thought. I explained that, with an energy field like that she would be perfect for the job. He asked me what I was talking about. It was at that moment, I realised that most other people do not see what I see. I remember clearly the feeling of feeling the isolation.

The shock of that moment clearly now, several years on, wondering why, I had never realised before that I was alone in what I saw, most of the time. I knew others did not see and hear the spirits I saw, but, for others not to see energy fields shocked me. I was thirty six years old and still learning much about my gifts and myself. A bigger learning curve was just around the corner.

Expect the Unexpected

"No-one expects...... the Spanish Inquisition"

Monty Python's Flying Circus

Being health conscious, every year George attended a private clinic for a medical. As is procedure with men over a certain age, he had had a blood test to check PSA count. The test is a possible indicator of prostate cancer.

The test is highly controversial, thus, we initially ignored the advice of the private doctor; that we should contact his GP (General Practitioner/doctor). George had no symptoms of prostate cancer and seemed fit and healthy. However, for whatever reason, George eventually thought it wise to visit the GP who forwarded the results to the hospital.

The usual biopsies were taken and we both visited the hospital for the results. We were expecting to be given the all clear. We should have realised something was wrong, when all the other patients went in to the consulting room before us; despite them arriving later than ourselves. A major fear of mine, from being a young girl, was that I would be a widow.

We were coolly welcomed into the office and the specialist got straight to the point.

"You have cancer Mr G; we recommend surgery as soon as possible as your cancer count is six. It could spread into the surrounding area anytime soon. You have about ten years if you

151

don't have surgery, I do not advise chemo, and neither would I advise radiotherapy. We need a decision within the next few weeks, so you and your partner can have time to think about things".

He then proceeded to explain about the procedure, recovery rates, possible complications, etc. My brain went into overdrive, what was happening? Surely there was a mistake? Our life was so wonderful, we were so happy, surely this was NOT happening?

I had waited for this perfect love, all my life, now it seemed it could disappear, swallowed into the abyss of nothingness. I felt as though I would die. This cool, calm consultant was so matter-of-fact, so detached. Had he any idea what he was saying? The implications of such a diagnosis were too catastrophic!

I began crying and shaking uncontrollably. Every cell in my body screamed 'despair' at me. The ultimate realisation that this man, whom I loved dearly, this man who was my whole life, was in fact about to die. Without warning I began wailing and rocking back and forth. My usual calm demeanour left without a trace. I was completely consumed with grief and fear.

"You've made a mistake!" I blurted, through a massive torrent of sobs and tears. "We've only just found one another; you can't take him from me now! I can't live without him!" The hospital staff were caught off their guard. They searched the small consulting room for tissues, taken by surprise by this deranged, mad woman who continued to rant. . . on and on.

How could this be happening? Why hadn't I seen it? I am a psychic and a healer yet I had had no inclination or warning, of this devastating explosion that I had just stepped into. My head ached and my body felt as though it didn't belong to me. Why was this happening to us? What had we done to deserve THIS?

Meanwhile George handled the situation admirably, calmly and explained that we would inform them of our decision as soon as possible. They apologised and subsequently went on to explain, that the tears usually come when the second consultation gets underway, not in the initial consultation!!!

We left the hospital that evening, hand in hand. I was still crying and sobbing, I was aware of people within the hospital looking at me and wondering what on earth was happening. I remember catching my breath wherever possible, before starting all over again.

I was in NO fit state to go home. I'd promised that whatever the outcome of that consultation I would drive home. I wasn't fit for anything!!! I told George that I couldn't face going home to the children. They were all so in-tune with me that they would know instantly, I was completely in bits. They would have got into a massive panic which would worsen everything.

We needed a detour and a support network. It was agreed that we would go to Marianne's house. She was shocked at the way I had reacted. I am usually a calm person and in control of my emotions, dealing with issues as they arrive. I was known, and respected, for taking charge of stressful situations. Yet, here I was, a complete emotional wreck.

She had known that we were attending the hospital that day for the results of the tests. However, upon seeing me, she didn't know whether to slap me or to hug me. Luckily she hugged me. In her presence and with her words of wisdom and kindly support, I began to calm. George was still calm and in total charge of his feelings. Looking back, the emotions of that day are as raw as they ever were. There are some things in life that we never forget.

We agreed surgery was probably the best option, especially as his cancer count was high. It could spread to the surrounding areas at any time. Thank goodness that I could practically apply the healing, and do something constructive to get through this incredibly, stressful time. We each were treated by our homeopath for shock and trauma, which helped massively in our time of need.

Every night leading up to the surgery, I did healing on George. It deepened our love in the relationship and it helped us to cope. It provided quiet time for both of us to share our thoughts. It also created focus and strength for us both. We knew the surgery carried risks, the risk of general anaesthetic, surgery itself, it felt as though we had no choice, other than to trust, that all would eventually be well.

Two weeks before the date of the operation, I suggested that we have a short break in the Lakes – to our beloved Wastwater. George had hardly ever been ill in his life. Most of us say we work fully on all six batteries, George ran constantly on twelve! He had no idea what it would be like to recover after major surgery.

Whilst walking, he confided his worst fears that he may not recover, that he may have no energy and be weak. I loved him regardless, and constantly assured him that we would face it together, all would be well. If allopathic/conventional medicine couldn't work, I knew enough healers and therapists to find someone; or several, to get him well again.

It was obvious that, for the first time in his life, he was very scared. Luckily, by this time, I had found an inner strength that I didn't know I had previously. We enjoyed the break, despite having the black cloud hanging over us. It was very unnerving to know that, within a few days of our arriving at home, we were going to face the vast unknown.

The morning of the operation was very emotional for us all. We had to be on the hospital ward by seven o'clock. The bag was packed and placed in the car. George was in tears, as the children came to say "goodbye and good luck". He had already made it clear, the only visitors he wanted there, whilst in hospital, would be me and his friend Philip. He was vulnerable and extremely nervous. Now it was my turn to remain strong.

The tension in the car on the way to the hospital was tangible. The combination of knowing that we would be separated, (he was expected to be in hospital for several days), the fear of not knowing what was to come, and the concern regarding the extent of his recovery, weighed like heavy boulders on our hearts. The totality of the situation had finally arrived.

We arrived in good time and despite that fact that I was falling apart inside, I managed to keep a brave face for him. It was incredibly stressful, waiting for a bed, filling out forms, further last minute examinations, etc. How I wanted it all to be okay. How I wanted this not to be happening. How I wanted to run away. How I desperately wanted it all to be one big horrible dream and how I wanted it all to go away.

George was finally allocated his bed, given his name tag and less than sexy surgical gown. His eyes showed me the volume of fear was ever increasing. I constantly reassured him and agreed that I would go down to the operating theatre with him. Promising that I would be there when we awoke, and that I would stay, as long as I was allowed, was easy for me. He would soon be home and, with all the healing and tender loving care, he would make a full and wonderful recovery.

Each step felt like an eternity, as he was finally wheeled down to theatre. The staff who greeted us were very kind, although we were both so very, very scared. As the anaesthetic was administered George drifted off. This was it, the time had come and it was NOW.

The strength I had had now totally dissipated. I felt so alone and fear crept into every cell of my being. Some days before the hospitalisation, my dear friend Marie, had suggested, that whilst George was in theatre, she would stay with me. I had to telephone her; I was desperate for a friendly face. I remember standing in the hospital car park, crying and sobbing so much, that she could hardly understand a word I said.

There were many risks to the surgery and I was terrified that I would lose him. She stayed with me, offering unconditional love and support as she listened to my fears and concerns. I am forever grateful, that she had the insight, to suggest that she stay with me during those fretful hours. Eventually, the time came, when the staff suggested I be back on the ward.

George returned from theatre and was obviously in pain, and a little groggy. I stayed all day and vowed to return the following day. It was a very long week; being parted, worrying about him, jumping every time the phone rang, sleepless nights and the worry of how he would recover once he got home.

The day before he was discharged I arrived to find him in tears. His eyes were bloodshot and it was obvious that he had been crying for hours. He was in an absolutely desperate emotional state. The fear, trauma, uncertainty of his recovery, the pain and the extent of his vulnerability, following major surgery had finally compounded into a huge torrent of emotions.

I held him and offered my support whilst he explained, "I don't care about the business; I just want you and the boys. Nothing else in my life matters." He was in such a desperate state. I had never seen him so vulnerable and it shocked me. He continued to cry and it wasn't until the early hours of the following morning, that he eventually started to calm.

Seeing a grown man cry is very humbling indeed. Seeing my beloved George emotionally in pieces was absolutely heartbreaking. I can still see his face and recall the panic, fear and the shock as the volume of these combined emotions held him in a vice-like grip.

We were delighted when, eventually he was told he could come home. I put plenty of cushions in the car, so he would be comfortable and was so pleased that finally he would be home. I was nervous too. He had had major surgery and things could still go wrong.

As we walked down the corridor his pace was very slow and he panicked if anyone came anywhere near him. The fear of someone banging into his wound was very apparent indeed. It was obvious just how exhausted he still felt too. Eventually we made it to the car and he eased himself in very, very gently. At last we were together again.

The nurses had explained to me how to apply the dressings daily and all the other discharge information too, follow up appointments, etc. When we got home, he was tired and went straight to bed. He explained again that he didn't want any visitors for a few days. I remember making a brew when I got home that day and although he was home, was still very fragile. I would have to adjust and get used to a less than active George.

That night he was concerned that I might roll over and bang his wound in the night. I quickly reassured him that I would stay still & rigid and that he would be safe. It was so wonderful to have him home, yet, we both knew we were not quite out of the woods yet. We still had to wait for the results from the biopsies from the hospital and he would have to attend clinic for blood tests every six months.

Many of my friends are healers and they had all been sending their magic. This continued now he was home too. He stated clearly that he didn't want visitors so he relied on me for his care. Marianne telephoned daily to receive updates on his care and my family were very supportive.

The early days consisted of gently bathing him, helping him to get dressed and attending to his dressings. He would become very tense as I removed the old dressings and replaced the new. Following his discharge, in the first few days, he was weak and slept frequently during the day. As sleep is healing, this was an essential part of his recovery.

We had always been a busy couple, always doing something, walking, travelling or at that point, checking on the progress at the house. It was odd now to see him now, so tired and needy. It was also unusual for me to have time alone during the day whilst he slept. It was a huge time of adjustment for us both.

Several times each day I gave him homeopathic remedies, mostly arnica, hypericum and calendula which he took willingly, because he knew that this would speed up the healing process.

Also, at least once a day I sat with him, placing my hands within his energy field because his wound was too sore for me to put my hands physically on it. Each time I felt the healing energy pour into him. He also did his best to give himself healing too.

The hospital staff had advised that once he felt fit enough, he should walk a few paces daily in order to build his strength up gradually by walking around the local estate. He felt he had an action plan and day by day he lengthened the walks. I was amazed and pleased with his progress and determination to get well again. Often he would return from his walks and I recall being amazed at how far he had journeyed.

Several days later the staples were removed, easily and effortlessly. He was so relieved. Within the week, the doctor telephoned to check on his progress; "Are you okay Mr G, you have just had major surgery and I haven't seen you.... you haven't even requested a prescription for pain relief." The doctor was clearly surprised and confused. George swiftly concluded the conversation by saying that he was fine and didn't need any help.

The combination of homeopathy and healing, provided all the energy his body needed, to facilitate a full and very speedy recovery. To occupy his mind, he began to read again and even I was astonished at how quickly he recovered, being pretty mobile within two-three weeks. The healing and the homeopathy had done its work.

Being a creature of habit George wanted to return back to 'normality'. Always wanting progress, he was upset not being able to return to work on the farmhouse. We could merely oversee the works and visit daily to check how everything was progressing. For George this was frustrating, as was his having to rely on me and not being able to drive himself.

The Goldfish That Jumped

During his recovery, his brother and his wife invited us over to stay with them in France. Less than a month after surgery, we travelled over to France and though it fell to me to carry the luggage, no-one would have known that George had just had major surgery. It was to be a most welcome and much needed break, from everything. Their beautiful home overlooked the Pyrenees mountain range. It was all very familiar to me, again I knew I had lived near this village, or at least travelled through here in previous lives.

Whilst in France, he asked his brothers opinion and advice about returning to work in one of his businesses. He explained that profits were down and he was becoming very concerned. Two months later and fully recovered, he decided to return to work in his original company. Whilst we had been away profits had plummeted even more.

The Goldfish That Jumped

Back to Business

"When you are pushed pull. When you are pulled push. Find the natural course and bend with it, then you join with nature's power."

Dan Millman

Profits had fallen hugely, the staff were all in desperate need of reassurance that things were going to improve and that their jobs were secure. Despite running my own business, the home with my children and overseeing the work on the farmhouse, I agreed to help. I had no idea what it would be like to work in a printing company. I knew I had much to learn, though I also knew that it would present me with a huge challenge.

We both worked extremely hard to get the business back on track. We cleaned, painted, reassured the staff, talked to customers and did everything in our power to bring the business up to its maximum capacity. We visited many of the customers in the hope that we would establish why sales had spiralled downwards.

Conversations at home, always revolved around the business, and we talked about nothing else, other than how things could be improved. Even at the weekends, we would go in to the premises to do whatever we could to improve the productivity. We looked at every angle and checked through everything with a fine toothcomb. We both felt it was an uphill struggle, and then I became ill. I needed several days off and for a number of reasons felt I could not return.

We had very little time for ourselves at this time and certainly no quality time. Life had rapidly become all work and NO play. Whilst off work and poorly, I had time to reflect. I realised I had to slow down, concentrate on my own business and my family. So much had happened in such a short space of time and I was exhausted. George was almost at full strength again and threw himself into his work. Very little else seemed to matter to him.

At this time I still saw occasional clients and it really is amazing how The Universe often provides us with a reflection of our lives; in our clients and friends. A lady had come for a reading and she too had gone to help in her partners fashion outlet business. The people who worked in the business were deliberately conspiring to cause its downfall.

I couldn't believe what I was "seeing". She was most upset and, like me, felt that her partner was more interested in the business and his empire, than her or her children. They had been married for years and she was heart-broken. I gave her a healing too and we chatted easily. I listened to how she was feeling and, although couldn't share my story, felt relieved whilst I listened to her.

I was becoming aware that our relationship was under a great deal of pressure and the signs of the strain were beginning to show themselves, more and more. I knew I needed a break and time to heal.

By now I had a very keen interest in Homeopathy. I had seen the benefits with my own recovery following post viral fatigue syndrome. I frequently used the remedies to treat myself, the children and even the cats. I had seen the amazing results with George following the cancer surgery too. All these factors combined, so I decided to attend a weekend seminar in The Lakes with Martin Miles; a well-respected and prominent homeopath.

I needed a break from everything that was going on at the time. I knew intuitively that it was the right thing for me, that

I attend the workshop. Maybe it would inspire me to study Homeopathy further?

George was so consumed with the printing business, that we agreed I would attend the weekend seminar alone. I hoped the respite might even give us both a chance to realise, how much we missed one another when we were apart.

In the early hours of that Saturday morning, I set off, feeling really excited to be looking forward to doing something for myself. I love the Lake District and I enjoy driving too. My friend Julie was with me and it was lovely to catch up and enjoy some female company. We arrived at the bed & breakfast and then went on to the college in Ambleside. The atmosphere was so calm and Martin's passion for Homeopathy and his attitude to teaching proved to me immediately that I had made the right choice.

That evening, after Julie and I enjoyed a meal at the local public house, we walked by the lakeside. She had seen our relationship deteriorate and she too, was confused as to what had suddenly changed. I needed my closest friend's advice and we chatted until the early hours. I was missing George and hoped that he too, was missing me.

The following morning we drove through the beautiful scenery, past the lakeside to the college. Another warm welcome greeted us and we were again provided with so much knowledge and wisdom. The other attendees and staff members were so friendly, many of whom were from a medical background, disillusioned by conventional medicine.

Martin had been a homeopath for years and had recently been proving (making), some new remedies. As he described the results of one case study after another, I was filled with his enthusiasm. The results when he prescribed these for his patients were awesome. His patients had returned to health very quickly, being fully healed.

The seminars inspired me and the whole experience was so positive, allowing me, without doubt, to make a decision which would be life-enhancing. Without hesitation, I signed up for a three year course at The Lakeland College of Homeopathy.

The weekend proved to be successful for me in many ways, especially as I would meet many new friends who would, over time, provide me with an incredible amount of support and healing. Little did I know at the time, how powerful that three year course would prove to be, in allowing me to look within myself, even deeper than I had done previously.

Slowly, slowly, despite my best efforts, over the coming year, our relationship continued to deteriorate. I usually rise to a challenge and am always optimistic. I loved George dearly and, without hesitation, I continued to keep hope and tried so very hard to keep our love alive. It was fast becoming an uphill struggle though; one which kept taking unexpected twists and turns.

It felt as though I was alone in realising what was happening and he became ever more distant from me. We communicated less and less and over time he stopped laughing, smiling and joking. Watching the man I so loved deteriorate, withdraw from me and the outside world was one of the hardest things I have ever done in my life.

I became very fearful as I had sold my own house and had moved in with George. The economic climate had recently changed, house prices had risen sharply and my business had just pottered along. I knew I couldn't afford financially to stay in this huge farmhouse without Georges' assistance. I also knew that as we were merely co-habiting, legally, I had no rights to the house.

No matter how often I tried to communicate my feelings to George, I was aware things were spiralling downwards rapidly. My sons lived with us, so it would mean setting up a new home, mortgage, re-establishing my business and starting all over again.

As if these stresses were not enough, these awful feelings of worry and concern constantly ran through my being. Worst of all, the man that I truly loved, was becoming ever consumed with more and more business worries. This, I guess, was probably a major reason why he was becoming more and more distant from me. Who knows?

The love that I had craved throughout my life was becoming more and more distant. Just like sand runs through your fingers, everything I had ever wanted was ebbing away very, very fast and I had no control of the situation.

Thoughts of fear were running through my head constantly. The potential reality of leaving my dear partner, someone whom I had felt was my best friend consumed me. Leaving him would mean that my life would change forever. If I left, there would be no going back. I would have to leave my home too.

I felt as though I were between a rock and a very hard place. Living with him and watching him spiral down was awful. Leaving him was something that I had never envisaged. We were all attached to George and had at one time been incredibly close to him. Now, not only was he distant with me, but, he was also very distant with them too.

My sons approached me frequently, expressing their concerns for his welfare. This compounded the guilt I felt at having made yet another mistake in life's tapestry. What would people think of me? I felt useless and disempowered. I spent hours feeling sorry for myself, and the guilt weighed me down like a lead balloon. I needed to take stock and re-evaluate my life.

The Universe, as always, had the situation under control and one damp, miserable October afternoon, I broke the Malleolus bone in my foot. The Universe was giving me an opportunity to slow down and heal. I knew I had broken it, the instant I arose from having been sat on the floor. Oh, how it hurt and how noisy the cracking sound was too! However, the following day, when I initially visited casualty, they missed the broken bone on the X-ray.

It healed naturally, using both healing and a combination of remedies, for broken bones and soft tissue damage. Within three days, I was walking unaided on it. Ten days later, the hospital specialist telephoned, explaining that he had double-checked the x-ray. He apologised profusely, stating that the bone had clearly been broken.

The consultant asked how I was, and requested me to attend casualty to have the foot set in a cast. I explained that I was fine, it was still a little sore, though I was walking on it and managing well. He couldn't believe it when I walked in to the department unaided. He duly showed us the x-ray. The break was very clear indeed. He agreed to allow me home, without even so much as a tubi-grip. No cast was required and I was free to go to The Lakes for the weekend.

I had not paid close enough attention to the message from The Universe, to rest and heal. Sure enough, within two weeks was admitted to hospital with a serious kidney infection.

When we arrived home from having been away one Sunday evening, I felt a twinge in my back. It was very painful, yet, I was unable to understand why I was in so much pain. I hadn't stretched or pulled a muscle, lifted anything, etc. I retired to bed much earlier than normal that evening, feeling absolutely exhausted.

The following morning, the pain was much worse. I awoke, and, as regular as clockwork, got up and sorted out the children, then made breakfast for George and the family. I felt quite tired though and weak. My usual sparkle had abandoned me. In fact, when they had all left for the day, I returned to bed.

The pain became increasingly worse and again, I searched my brain for what I had done, to cause this amount of discomfort. I failed to sleep, due to the pain, although I managed a light doze. Within a couple of hours I needed the loo and, when I tried to get out of bed, I almost passed out.

The Goldfish That Jumped

The pain when I moved was excruciatingly painful. I fell back onto the bed, in agony and confusion. I felt as though I was freezing cold too. This is a classic symptom of a very high temperature. Having studied biology and having a keen interest in medicine, I realised that I was in trouble and needed urgent medical assistance. I needed a doctor as soon as possible.

Living in a huge farmhouse meant that whichever route I chose, I had quite a walk to get to one of the three external doors. I needed a plan, and I needed to think fast as I knew I was deteriorating rapidly.

Luckily, the telephone was by the bed. I called the doctor, praying fervently that it would be answered by an understanding receptionist. I hadn't even been to our doctors, as I was usually so fit and healthy. I described my symptoms and explained that I needed a home visit, from a doctor, urgently.

She must have recognised the panic in my voice and she immediately put me through to a doctor. I explained how ill I felt, and that, under the circumstances, I would leave the door open, assuming I had enough energy to get downstairs to the door. Having three external doors in this huge property, meant that I had to explain, very clearly, which one would be open.

As I replaced the receiver, I suddenly became very, very scared. I knew I would need hospitalisation and, as George was already extremely stressed, wondered how I would explain it to him. When he had last seen me, less than three hours previously, I had been in pain; but not in agony like this.

I telephoned him and luckily he was in the office. He agreed to come home urgently as I had stated that the doctor was on his way. I gingerly walked through the corridor and was exhausted by the time I got to the stairs. I gathered what little strength and stamina I had, knowing that I had to get to a main door. I prayed for help and endurance too. I honestly felt like I was about to die.

The pain was increasing in volume and momentum by the second, making me weaker and weaker. That day, getting down stairs was nothing less than a miracle. I staggered into the lounge and made my way through the hallway, at last I could unlock the door. Tears filled my eyes as the pain worsened. I was shivering as my temperature spiked higher and higher. Eventually, after what seemed an age, I made my way to the settee and lay there, frightened for my life.

Our kidneys represent fear. I knew I had a very serious kidney infection and I knew why. As I lay thinking about my life, I was scared. What would happen to me, I felt so very, very ill. My boys had left that morning and would now be told how ill I was. George had more than enough worries without me too. I honestly wondered if I would be dead before anyone found me.

George arrived home just a few minutes before the doctor called. The look of shock on seeing me said it all. Within a few moments, the doctor arrived and he recognised immediately how ill I was, and suggested that I go to hospital in an ambulance as I was unable to sit up. Besides being in agony, I felt I would pass out.

Later that day, in November 2006, I was admitted to hospital where I was monitored carefully. I recall very little of my admission, George said I was not really coherent. Within an hour, I was wired up on intravenous antibiotics and once stabilised, was moved to the ward.

I was in hospital for almost a week. I honestly do not recall much of that stay, although one night stands out clearly. I was desperate for the toilet and buzzed for assistance; as I had not got enough strength to walk myself to the cubicle. I explained to the healthcare assistant how ill I felt, begging her not to leave me alone. After relieving myself, I remember the room spinning.

That was my last memory. I was unconscious for some time, when I awoke a doctor named Thomas, was holding my hand. He stayed with me all night. I remembered dying that evening;

my grandfather came to me, surrounded in bright light and told me I must go back as it wasn't my time.

Our kidneys represent our fears. I was losing my best friend and I was very, very frightened. My children were young adults, who no longer needed a mother as much as they had done in earlier years. My life held nothing as far as I could see, and I felt useless and abandoned. I had no future, no hope and my life was a wreck. I felt I was like a scared rabbit, running into the headlights, knowing at any time, I could be snuffed out.

After several days in hospital I was eventually discharged and allowed home. I was incredibly weakened and full recovery took several weeks. A dear friend stated that, years before, patients would have been sent to a convalescent home, for continued care and respite, rather than being sent home.

I have always been a strong woman, now I was weak and doing basic chores exhausted me. George had loved me for my strength, now I had nothing left to give, and his "Superwoman" was well and truly broken. I missed the first weekend course of Homeopathy, this too upset me even further.

George too was becoming ever more frustrated with me, and my continual tiredness. One night we had a huge row, things were said that I had bottled up for months. I explained I felt so bad that I was thinking of leaving. He explained that he had no idea at all, that things were so strained between us, and that I should have spoken up earlier. I had tried, but to no avail: hindsight is a wonderful thing.

I realise now that I hadn't communicated effectively to him, neither had I communicated the extent of my feelings with my ex-husband, nor in any previous relationships. I had just put up, allowing things to deteriorate further. This was a huge revelation to me and I would further comprehend the intensity of the learning over the following months, and indeed, subsequent years too.

He cried, then he sobbed, begging me not to leave. We agreed to become more aware of the others needs, to be more attentive to resolving the distance between us. We both wanted what we had we enjoyed in our relationship previously.

My first granddaughter was born to her delighted parents, within a week of my discharge from hospital. I was still very weak, although helped whenever I could and through this beautiful baby, my relationship with my daughter deepened. To this day, I recognise that I received so much love from this tiny being. I was able to give and receive so much from her, so much so that she gave me a renewed purpose in life.

Spending time with my daughter, son-in-law and the baby helped me to heal and gave me respite from the situation at home. Her birth was timed wonderfully and as I wasn't fit enough to work, gave me the chance to get to know her.

Despite frequent feelings of fear and terror of my unknown future, slowly I was finding the will to carry on. There was no way that I could ever leave her, my children, and extended family. I wanted so much to be there and to watch her grow up. To enjoy spending time and being there for her if she should ever need me, not to mention providing loving support to my daughter and son-in-law too.

The First Stage of Hell

"Nothing can hurt you unless you give it the power to do so"

A Course in Miracles

It was a very difficult time. The house was not quite finished, and the builders had done most of the work, though all the tricky little finishing touches needed to be done. We were constantly on the phone, virtually begging them to come and finish the work. The house in Samos was almost completed too, but the problems we were having in Britain, were very similar to those with the builders out in Greece.

There were problems with George's other businesses and he was becoming more and more stressed by the day. He had borrowed a huge amount of money, in order that we could finish work on the houses and finance his other businesses. I asked if we could down-size; I would have been happy to live anywhere with him.

Who knows what the reason, or reasons were. He began to shut me out, even more than he had previously, eventually pushing me further and further away, so that there was to be no return.

We tried counselling, and even the counsellor refused to work with him on three occasions – he was so distant. After the first counselling session we both suffered from tonsillitis and laryngitis. Neither of us could speak and both us of were ill. The counselling had unearthed so much miscommunication. I can honestly say that the deterioration of the relationship was the worst thing that I had ever experienced. It happened so quickly, it felt it was almost an overnight occurrence.

Previously we had often laughed and joked frequently, were very affectionate and appreciated one another totally, now there was nothing. He didn't even smile. One day we were together, the next we were not. I loved him dearly and tried everything I knew to get the old George back. It was futile and soul-destroying.

He became more interested in his businesses than me or the children. He wouldn't tell me what was wrong. We didn't share much quality time. He was always shattered. Even when we went to Greece he was so tired, stressed and distant he couldn't enjoy himself.

I dearly missed the man I had fallen in love with. Now, before me was a business man, consumed with making money and very little interest in anything else. We parted after almost four years. The morning I suggested that I move out, he glibly agreed. We both cried for hours; the first time I had seen any display of emotion from him for several months. It was heart-breaking.

When he eventually left to go to work that morning, I spent the day with friends, crying yet knowing that leaving the relationship was my only option. I couldn't live without him, but, living with him was killing me at a far faster pace. Thank goodness for friendships and support of those around us.

It was ironic, that when I returned home later that day, after visiting friends, he was sat outside waiting for me. His eyes were tearful and we chatted briefly. For the next three days, I could see there was a deep emotion within him. It seemed he was unsure, as to whether our separation would be right for him.

Later that week, he went away on business for two days. Upon his return the coldness returned, only by this time it was much more evident, than it had ever been before. The drawbridge was well and truly closed. There would be no going back, no more discussions and no further opportunities for possible resolution.

There was NO understanding on my part as to what had brought about this change and although we met six months after the split, neither of us had any answers as to what had gone wrong, in fact there was still an air of love between us. Unfortunately, there was not enough for me ever to return.

I love this quote from "Eat, Love, Pray" By Elizabeth Gilbert. It summed up exactly what had happened, and how broken, tattered and shredded my heart was at that time.

"A true soul mate is a mirror, the person who shows you everything that's holding you back, the person who brings you to your own attention so you can change your life. A true soul mate is probably the most important person you'll ever meet, because they tear down your walls and smack you awake............ they come into your life just to reveal another layer of yourself to you, and then they leave. They show you your obstacles and addictions, break your heart open so new light could get in, make you so desperate and out of control that you HAD to transform your life".

My soul mate and I were no more.

The Goldfish That Jumped

The Second Stage of Hell

"To forgive is the highest most beautiful form of love.

In return, you will receive untold peace and happiness"

Robert Muller

Now things had to change, I began to look for a house for me and the children. The boys were also upset and had seen the distance grow between us. In fact, one of my sons tried so hard to talk to him one afternoon, to explain how upsetting it was, to watch him become so distant from all of us - it was futile.

Once again I entered into the dark night of the Soul, only this time it was on a much deeper level. If I'd been there before, this new experience was The Beast of all Beasts. Most nights I lay awake covered in sweat, wondering what had gone wrong? I couldn't eat, and even struggled to drink.

There was nothing I wouldn't have done for George. I loved him for all that he was, his good, bad and his in between points. The love was unconditional and without expectation. How was I going to live without this man in my life?

How could I ever leave him? Would he be okay? What would life be like without him? No longer would I be snuggling into him, wishing him "Good morning," no longer would we laugh and caress. I had lost any sense of a future. I also lost three stone in a matter of weeks. I was frequently in tears.

The Goldfish That Jumped

I needed to stay in the farmhouse, at least until I had purchased my new home. It was an extremely difficult time. We ate together and just didn't talk or communicate. Being a big house, the boys and I lived in one part and he stayed in another.

Throughout most of the summer, he spent time in Greece. I felt this was so he wouldn't have to face the fact that we were leaving. Neither did he have to face the subsequent fall out. I had the house to myself, much of the time. He didn't tell me where he was going or when he would return. It was awful to watch this brokenness. And, it was awful for me to experience mine.

I asked the Universe for healing; for the situation and for the two of us. I kept trying to talk with him – all to no avail. Then overnight, several weeks later, something changed and there was a chance for us to talk. I was due to move out within a fortnight, so it was a huge relief to feel there was no longer such a huge river between us.

We still had no answers for what had happened, but at least the children and I left on speaking terms to him. The final weekend, before I was moving into my new home he spoke some of the most profound words to me;

"I know far more than I am cracking on, you have much more work to do and many people to touch.
I am only holding you back. I know I have to let you go".

The words touched my soul and I knew there was no going back. They seemed to come from someone else. Maybe they were channelled, I really don't know – but, I remember it clearly and I recall that even his voice was different, whilst he spoke these powerful words.

Moving On (Again)

"We are all on a spiral path. No growth takes place in a straight line. There will be setbacks along the way....
There will be shadows, but they will be balanced by patches of light and fountains of joy as we grow and progress.
Awareness of the pattern is all you need to sustain you along the way."

Kristin Zambucka

The day we agreed to separate, I knew I needed to look for a new home. Ironically, I also knew I needed to go into the same estate agents where the farmhouse had been advertised. I saw the advert for what has become our new home on my first visit. Due to difficult circumstances with the seller, it hadn't been possible for me to view the property initially.

Several days later when I approached the garden, the voice of my spirit guide stated, very loudly "Home". As I walked down the front path, the voice continued "Home...... this will be a very happy home". I was rather dumbstruck, as the owner opened the door.

I was shown around and knew I would live here with my children. Things were a little slow to progress, as the owner had several domestic issues to resolve. In November 2007, with the help of friends, we eventually moved in. It was an incredibly emotional day. We all felt it was very odd to move from such a huge farmhouse, into a much smaller property. However, we soon made it homely, and I knew it was the right thing to do, for both me and my sons.

Despite having been in business myself for several years, during the time I was with George, I honestly hadn't put the effort into things. I had become distracted, helping him in his businesses and wanting to spend time with him; especially after the cancer diagnosis; as both life and time were precious.

Converting the properties took up much time and, in all honesty, I had thought that was to be my future, so, investing the time in these things, had obviously seemed the right thing to do, at the time. I had almost totally disempowered myself. I had sold my own home when I moved in and now needed to rebuild the business, me and my life.

Practically, the house was in need of many improvements. The kitchen was outdated and filthy. The walls were of bare plaster, so needed a lick of paint. In what was to become my bedroom, the ceiling and walls needed re-plastering and completely rebuilding. The garden was a mass of weeds and overgrown shrubbery. My sons and my father were a great help.

Whilst coping with all these changes, I was still in shock; grieving for the lost relationship. Every day I thought about George and hoped he was well. I wondered if he, or I, would ever love again. I wondered, if the huge hole in my heart centre and, actually in my life, would ever heal. I had to grow my business again, apply myself and move on.

I decided to cash in all my savings, in order that we could pay for the necessary household improvements and repairs. As we began one job, it became clear that the previous work on the house had been done with very little attention to quality. It was a steep, and very expensive, learning curve.

To be honest, looking back I don't know how I got through. We managed to make the house a very welcoming home and my business grew quickly too. My head was still well and truly up my back-side, but, day by day I managed. My friends and family supported me in every way and for that I am forever grateful.

Through my work, I made many new friends. Some more prominent than others, but, nonetheless, I received a lot of help. My family were wonderful, my parents and children too. My granddaughter was my rock, and, watching her develop gave me great pleasure. The business went from strength to strength. My remaining savings gave me some flexibility, allowing me to visit my beloved Italy, Ibiza and Iona too.

Looking back, the first year after the split was the worst. Then, slowly, I began to get stronger. As I grew in strength and understanding of myself, I gradually let go of the questions that had been running through my head. What went wrong? Could I have done anything more? Should I have tried for longer? What had happened …….. round and round like a goldfish in its bowl!!!

The Homeopathy played a major role in my healing process. Attending college, in Ambleside, in The Lake District, one weekend every month, created a distraction from my emotional pain. There are many remedies for loss and grief; I was probably prescribed every one!

The Lakes gave me back a focus in life. The beautiful scenery, the tutors and students alike, helped with my emotional recovery. The weekend course started at 9.30am, I am a very early bird, so I usually set off on my journey before 7.30am. As I have done earth healing work from a very tender age, I thought it would be a good idea to make time to spend by Bowness each month.

This would allow me to balance the energies in the surrounding area. I would make up a flask and stand by the lake, checking, and then balancing the energies. I thoroughly enjoyed this most quiet and, very precious start to my day. Feeding the ducks, swans and wildfowl added so much to the pleasure to the weekend. This became *me* time and to be honest was very special to me indeed.

I was instructed by my guides whenever the energies in The Lakes were imbalanced. If I needed to travel to do the healing work I would always find the time and found the process very rewarding. Though a slow process, I was healing and rebuilding my life at last.

The Lakeland College in Ambleside had proven to be a rock for me. Providing a safe haven where I could look honestly at myself and grow. Ambleside itself, the trees and surrounding mountains, proved to be a huge part in my healing process. I now include Homeopathy in my practise and have had many successes.

Learning about the remedies, flower essences, energy work, animal essences and a multitude of medical data, was a joy for me. In order to graduate, we attended clinics and tutorials, they each added their own magic to the experience. As a group, the girls were wonderfully supportive, and, we would all contact one another in between the weekends of lectures. I am very blessed to have such a fabulous group of friends.

I graduated in the summer of 2009. My wonderful family and closest friends were with me that weekend. As part of the celebrations, we were each given framed photographs of The Lakes. Mine was a magnificent picture of Castlerigg stone circle, near Keswick. It was a place that had, by now, become so very dear to me. A place where I *had grown and healed so much,* helping me to flower; a place where I had also experienced so much past life déjà vu.

No-one at the college, knew of the huge significance Castlerigg held for me. Out of all the other possible scenic pictures of The Lakes, that I could have been given, I was given my absolute souls space. I treasure the picture to this day and always will.

Another chapter in my life was completed; yet at the same time, creating a space for another to begin.

Friendships Through Lifetimes

"What comes from the heart touches the heart"

Don Sibet

In early November, my guides requested that I visit Wastwater, as the ley lines needed balancing. Always willing, I rearranged my diary, mentioned to close friends Kate and Diane that I was going away, and promptly packed up my holdall, to include waterproofs & thermals, of course! My friends asked if they could come with me, and if so, would I show them how to work with the ley lines.

This seemed like a good idea and we set off towards Wasdale. Kate's relatives had property in the local area and we agreed to stay in Kendal. It was lovely and we arrived at the far end of Wastwater Lake. Neither Kate nor Diane had been to the area before, so they were absolutely thrilled as the scenery is incredibly stunning and beautiful.

Wastwater is the deepest of all the lakes and the surrounding mountains are magnificent too. The whole area is amazing and is unlike any other part of the Lake District. The locals say it even has its own ecosystem, I certainly agree, as the weather here can change rapidly.

The whole area has an energy which is very unique, one that is tangible to most people, whether or not they class themselves as sensitive. At the end of the lake is a tiny chapel, which is an absolute favourite of mine. Surrounded by yew trees and wilderness, it really is a remarkably peaceful, deeply spiritual place. They loved everything about the whole valley, particularly the chapel, and were deeply touched, on a soul to soul level.

We had enjoyed the drive into this magical valley. When we arrived by the lakeside, I showed them how to do the healing work. Both found the work easy and enjoyed helping me. I was deeply moved too and it was wonderful to share places with those we love.

That night it was great to have girlie company and our stay was very comfortable. However, I began to feel unsettled and was unsure as to why. As I explained, I often become aware of pending disasters, before they happen.

This night, I felt most unsettled, so I assumed that this was probably the case. I sent healing energy and allowed it to go wherever it was needed; thinking it was an imbalance of energy somewhere, or an international disaster. I could not have been more wrong.

The following morning, the feeling of unrest still remained, which was most unusual. I pretended I was okay but, as the morning progressed my friend knew something was wrong. She insisted that she knew I felt uneasy and try as I might she was not having my feeble excuses.

Eventually, I admitted I felt absolutely awful, with intense unease. In fact, I further explained that when I tuned in to the feeling, I felt that someone close to me was about to leave the Earth plane. I was unsure who it was, and obviously this in itself is unsettling, as it can be someone very close. I explained that no matter how much healing I sent I felt dreadful.

She agreed to send me some healing and we continued through Kendal enjoying the day. We left for home late that afternoon. I had patients booked in for appointments that evening. My first arrived and my second client cancelled. I was still feeling very uneasy and decided to phone my friend Sam.

The Goldfish That Jumped

He was a shaman and I had learnt much from him. He intuited from my voice that I was feeling uncomfortable. I explained that I had felt that someone close to me was about to die. "Ummmm" was the reply, which I knew meant that he knew far more than he was telling me!!!

As we spoke a "figure" appeared on my plinth (massage couch). I could see him clearly. This is known as astral projection. Sam asked me to describe him, and go down the body, feeling what was wrong with this person. I described his stature .... over six feet tall and very, very broad, short dark hair and someone in very poor health.

Sam obviously knew who this person was, and went on to explain that his name was Pierre. He was suffering from motor neurone disease and wasn't expected to live until New Year. It was actually very doubtful, whether or not he would make it to Christmas at all.

Pierre had appeared to other healers too, they had all suspected that there was another member of the soul group, whom he would seek out. I had never physically met this man and just felt that I was here to offer healing, support and comfort.

The more healing I sent, the more the unsettling sensation disappeared. It was such a relief. After feeling agitated for over 24 hours, finally, I could relax. I communicated with Pierre, that he was "welcome to stay" and receive healing as long as he liked. He stayed for three days and reappeared randomly following this initial meeting.

This form of healing is known as astral projection. The soul leaves the physical body and travels elsewhere for healing, or communication. Many examples of this exist, often when someone is about to die, no matter what physical distance may be between people, the person appears to others, sometimes several people at once, then dies a few minutes later or is seen at the time of death.

Often when we have had a very "real" dream, we have astral-projected out of our bodies. This is usually why we feel very spacey in the morning, just as we awaken. The soul has left the body and now needs to be reconciled within the physical density of our physical form.

Sam called me daily to check whether or not Pierre was still receiving healing from me. He explained that they had been friends for many years. Pierre was a fellow healer, having many like-minded friends. I was told he was wheel-chair bound, as the disease had consumed him so much, that he could only move certain fingers, and his head. His speech was weakened and slurred.

Sam agreed that we should meet, explaining that he had suspected for some time, that Pierre and I knew one another. It certainly wasn't from this lifetime, though I knew I had to meet him. It was all arranged for the 21st December 2008.

When the day finally came, I was very excited, yet very, very nervous at the same time. Sam had explained to me that there would be thirteen of us in total. I only knew Sam and felt a "knowing" of Pierre, so was daunted at the thought of meeting twelve strangers. Nonetheless I knew I had to be there, and wondered what it would be like, to finally meet this man in the physical sense.

It was a surreal experience and one I will never forget. We arrived on time and were greeted at the door by fellow healers. They had all known I would be attending, beforehand, though I really was unaware of them. Yet, in the first few moments of meeting all twelve people for the first time, we all knew we knew one another and we all got on as though we had known one another for years.

Pierre was sat by the window in the lounge, in his wheelchair. It was a magical and very touching moment, when our eyes met I felt I had known him forever. It was a mixed emotion of joy, shock and sadness, because I knew we didn't have long to get to know one another. We hugged and hugged, I was unable to prevent the tears from running down my cheeks.

We chatted easily about all things, healing, our "odd" meeting, our peculiar knowing of one another too. He explained that he was most grateful for the relief the healing brought, whilst at the same time, being fully aware that he was doing the astral travel. He asked if I minded his visits. I explained that he usually chose to appear when I was teaching, and, that many of my students had seen and felt his presence too.

He smiled a most warming smile, one that I will never forget. I can still recall that moment clearly, filled with emotional charge, as I write this paragraph. It was very clear then, and I realize now, how deeply moved I was to meet this man.

We all celebrated the Winter solstice together with a wonderful Christmas lunch. I left that evening knowing that my soul had indeed been well and truly touched. I was amazed at the generosity of people sharing their home with me, and their food, those who had previously been total strangers. An experience I will always treasure.

Sam and I often saw Pierre weekly following that event. We chatted and laughed sharing many experiences and sharing our déjà vu. We had had many past life memories and being in his presence allowed and encouraged me to re-experience them.

I have known for years that I have had lifetimes as a Native American Indian medicine woman. I have also had many lifetimes as a male: that's why I am tall and broad. Yet, prior to meeting Pierre, I had been unaware that I had been a Native American warrior. I recalled that I was his brother in this particular lifetime.

I had been away travelling, when I got the news that he was very seriously ill and in fact, close to death. As a mighty warrior, I always felt that I had to be strong. A warrior was taught not to cry and so, when I got the news that my brother was dying; although it would have been easy for me to travel back to the village and spend the last hours with him, I deliberately stalled, not being able to let down my guard and experience my vulnerability.

The emotions were incredibly powerful and the recollection very vivid. I arrived at the village, less than an hour after Pierre had died; as I felt this would spare me my pain. How foolish I was. Upon seeing his dead body, I let out a scream of emotional torture and realized that I should have been there for my kin.

I should have put down my emotions and put my brothers' needs first. He was dying after all. I was not a warrior now; I was a human being, now bereft and full of guilt. I vowed I would be there next time, and would never again allow my pride to come in between my humanness again. This is why Pierre had sought me out in this lifetime, so we wouldn't repeat the same mistake again.

Meeting Pierre allowed me to further my déjà vu and deepen my awareness. Whenever, we met, both he and Sam spoke in fluent Native American Indian tongue. The language was very lovely to listen to and, the strange thing being, that often I just knew what they were saying to one another.

It was very bizarre indeed and the meetings would always bring up further learning for me. One particular day I went to visit Pierre alone and as we sat together he said "whenever I look into your eyes I can go anywhere in the world. Thank you for being you." It was so touching and we shared so many things, experiences of healing, how we re-awakened, to name but few.

He was not expected to survive much beyond Christmas. However, he was still bright and cheery in May 2009. On this particular occasion, Sam, Kate and I visited him and within a few minutes, he had shape-shifted into an Atlantean Priest.

I was really dumb founded, as this allowed instant access to opening the flood gates with past live recall of that sacred time. Within moments, I recognised a deep anger within myself, towards Pierre. He smiled a smile of peaceful knowing; as he was already aware of what was to come.

The story quickly unfolded. We had been very great friends centuries ago, when he was a High Priest. I had fallen in love with him, and had after several months of soul-searching, decided that I would finally tell him the feelings I had for him.

He had invited me around that evening for a meal at his place and I was really excited. My thoughts were full of how he might respond to my honesty relating to my depth of feelings. Of course, I had also envisaged our first kiss. What it would feel like. Who would make the first move and was looking forward to at last, letting go off these pent up emotions.

Immediately, when I arrived, and even before I had a chance to speak, he said he wanted to show me something. We left the house and wandered quite a way from our village, to a most secluded spot on a mountain. I thought he was being romantic, it was such a lovely place.

Here he found a concealed entrance in the stone. He gestured to me to follow him, when we went inside the mountain, we walked through narrow tunnels and passageways. We eventually came to a laboratory, where experiments relating to genetic modification were taking place. I was horrified and deeply distressed too. Time was being altered and worm-holes created. It was all right here, happening before my eyes.

I was absolutely mortified. The Ancient teachings of Atlantis were correct. He knew about these too, every student priest and priestess was encouraged to learn and obey these sacred wisdom teachings. Yet here he was, conducting and encouraging this inevitable destructiveness.

I ran from the cave, confused and feeling so very foolish too. The trauma of what I had just seen reeled through my whole being. I knew then that my beloved Atlantis would, in fact be destroyed. He knew I was livid at all that he had helped, and actually encouraged to create. I was both furious with him, and angry with myself, for allowing myself to fall in love with someone who, in my minds' eye, clearly had no respect for our teachings and our code of ethics.

The anger consumed my very being and the love I felt for him turned to absolute rage. As this déjà vu ran through every cell in my body. I was deeply saddened. Later that evening, my guides later gave me clear instructions to get a boat ready. Within a few days, I would be leaving the island…. alone.

This was heartbreaking news to me and meant I would be leaving my whole world behind and starting afresh. . . . I was being forced to leave a place of absolute beauty. Forced to leave all the things I held dear. I knew I would lose all I had ever loved there; the children I had taught, those I had brought into the world, my students and my dearest friends. My whole life was here. My future was now uncertain, though I was too angry to care.

Atlantis was meant to be destroyed as it had been written in the ancient scriptures. I realised that someone had to start the destructive sequence of events, now I knew and had an understanding of what had happened. It was all meant to be. I had to accept that in its entirety.

Sitting with Pierre, looking into his eyes and holding his hand tightly, I began to cry hysterically. For centuries, I had held on to that rage and fury. Now was the time to let it go and to appreciate, that it had all been meant to happen and acceptance was the key to peacefulness.

My bitter tears streamed down my face. I was crying tears of deep pain and sorrow. My heart centre ached and screamed out to me. My whole body was consumed with a deeper grief than anything, I had ever experienced previously. Through my tears, I knew I had to forgive my old friend Pierre. I also had to forgive myself, for holding onto the huge amounts of anger and rage.

I asked him to forgive me my anger and he just smiled acknowledging, all knowingly, that all was as it should be. That May Bank Holiday weekend, I cried for almost three whole days.

The déjà vu of Atlantis was incredibly clear and from that time many more memories began to unfold. The lesson learnt was anger and rage, bottled up for centuries and held against that *one* person. As the story unfolded, I realised I was angry with myself. Not the most pleasant of realisations, as I pride myself on my calmness and my placid manner.

That night I was given very clear instructions by my guides. I was told clearly to tell no-one, I would be leaving alone, under the cover of darkness, it was a very sad time indeed. As always, I followed their instructions without doubt, or question.

I got a small boat ready with supplies, as I had been directed, and hid it in the harbour of a very secluded cove. My whole being was weighted with deep grief and sadness. I knew the time would come very soon when I would be told to leave.

Several nights later the final instructions were given. I was to tell no-one I was leaving, get in the boat in the dead of night and take only water and a little food, no provisions or clothes were allowed.

As a High Priestess, I was known to everyone in the community and well-respected. No-one was permitted to know that I was about to leave. That night, I made an excuse that I would be meditating, and thus would be grateful, not to be disturbed. This was normal, so nobody suspected anything unusual, nor did anyone challenge me.

I awaited my guides' final instructions, as to the exact time I had to leave. I was still livid with Pierre, so much so, that I was not really concerned as to what would happen to me when I left. My discipline meant I was very capable of hiding my emotions, I didn't allow them to consume me. Yet, at this time it was incredibly difficult to pretend all was well. I was close to melt-down.

I had never rowed further than a few feet from the shore of the island. This was a whole new experience for me and one I didn't really want. To be honest, I no longer cared for my well-being. Everything I had ever valued, was about to be lost and taken from me. . . in my eyes at least.

My concern was for my children and peoples. I had asked my guides if I could stay and be destroyed alongside them. After all, isn't that what any leader would do? Their reply was swift and firm. I would leave and that was their final decision, there would be no compromise or alteration.

As I got into the boat, tears began to fall. I was sobbing as I cast off. I knew not where I was going and I actually didn't care. One by one, the faces of those I held dear consumed my being and I said a quiet prayer for each and every one of them.

I loved all my people and knew each by their name. We had all shared so many wonderful experiences. The birth and deaths of loved ones, nature's celebrations, rather like harvest festivals of today, etc. We were a loving and very close community. I couldn't imagine what life would be without them.

I sailed in the dead of night, as I got further from the shoreline the lights from the mainland became much smaller. There was a cool breeze and I pulled my robe closer. Although my guides gave me reassurance, I was consumed with a swirl of so many powerful emotions, that I dismissed them. I was angry with them too, in fact, it felt like I was angry with the whole world.

The sound of the water lapping against the boat was soothing, almost hypnotic. Eventually I drifted off to sleep. I had no idea where I was or where I was going. Our sacred teachings held information relating to other civilisations and places, but I had never really paid any attention, as I had always felt I would stay on the island.

The Goldfish That Jumped

As I slept, I knew my guides would keep me safe, as the boat rocked from side to side. It was a restless sleep, memories and faces all jumbled into one. When I awoke the following morning I was surrounded by ocean, drifting aimlessly at sea. I knew there was no going back and I gave more and more control to the anger, allowing it to consume the whole of my being.

Any instructions my guides gave to me became clouded and blurred, whereas before I had always known absolute clarity. I rowed the oars, though my arms were by now very tired and my hands were blistering. I was losing touch with my soul and I knew it. Up until now, throughout my whole life, I had lived with discipline. I taught the value of the soul connections with guides and with Source, now I didn't care. The more anger I felt, the more distance I created between me and my inner essence.

As far as I remember, I had been at sea for several days when a huge wave almost threw me overboard. I knew it was the aftermath of the tsunami that had claimed the lives of my peoples. I felt I had abandoned them in their hour of need, and although my guides were trying to communicate to me that this was not the case, I felt I had betrayed them.

More tears fell and by now I had exhausted my food supplies and had very little water left. I didn't feel much like a healer, a priestess, nor did I feel wise. I fell asleep, overwhelmed by emotions and shock too.

Eventually, two or three days later the tiny boat was beached on another island. I was very weak and struggled to get out of the vessel. My hands were raw of skin, after rowing for so long. I wandered around in a daze and shouted at my guides: "Why have you left me here, why didn't you just allow me to die? Why me, why would an Atlantean priestess with all her knowledge and wisdom, be abandoned on this god-forsaken island without any inhabitants?"

For the first time in days, I listened as they guided me gently to a source of fresh water and advised me which fruits I could eat, and how to open them. Tasting the fresh water was lovely and soothed my parched mouth and lips. They also showed me which plants leaves I could place on my hands, to soothe the pain.

I calmed a little as I washed, drank and ate. I rested awhile, gathering a little strength, before I wandered onto the beach. I had no idea how to make a shelter, or where to find a shelter. My guides told me it was all taken care of, that I should just enjoy the new surroundings. I grunted back.

Several hours passed and the sun was beginning to go down. It was still remarkably warm and I welcomed the coolness. I wandered by the beach and calmed as I watched the waves ebb and flow. They were almost mesmerizing and I sent a healing prayer up for my lost peoples. Pictures and thoughts of them, happy memories played through my mind. I sat by the shoreline day-dreaming.

I thought I was hearing things when I heard my name being called. "Mary, Mary, welcome to our island." How did they know my name? Surely I was hearing things? It was all rather strange to me. As I turned towards the voices, I saw a crowd of people approaching.

They knew I was here and they also knew my name. As the leader approached, I saw his gentle facial features and welcoming smile. He was a tall man, at least 10-15 years older than me. He had a kind, loving face and a beautiful, light bright energy field; displaying compassion and wisdom.

He was very obviously very spiritual, and greeted me with open arms and a welcoming smile. He introduced himself as William, and introduced me to his peoples. They could see by my facial expression that I was surprised, that they had known I was coming and my name. As they came closer, it was clear that they were all genuinely pleased to see me.

Their leader explained that my coming had been expected for months. They had eagerly awaited my arrival, as they knew of my healing capabilities. Their healer had passed over many months before, and no-one had been capable of healing in such a profound way.

They had requested help from the guardians and were told of my coming. So I was naturally to step into my role of healer and teacher again. They gently guided me with them on a path through the trees lining the beach. I was welcomed into their village. A hut had been made ready for me. It was very homely indeed and I was overcome by their ability to make me feel at ease.

Over the coming days, I was introduced to those who needed healing and women with children, young babies and those with child. My midwifery skills would soon be needed. I quickly fitted into the community and within a few weeks each of them knew me personally. They would freely ask advice and help relating to health and well-being.

Within a short space of time, I was holding workshops and talks about chakras and healing generally. I loved my new life, but inside a well of rage was still gathering pace. I missed my old community and still felt that I had betrayed them in many ways. Here I was, in a new life and actually beginning to settle and enjoy myself.

Despite the teachings saying that Atlantis would be destroyed, and knowing that everything happens at the right time, for the right reason, I was fighting my own internal turmoil. I was no longer the leader and this gave me a reason and a place to focus my anger.

William, their leader was a lovely soul, of that there could be no doubt, and he deserved to be the leader. However, as the anger raged silently underneath my pleasant exterior, I yearned for my leadership to be returned to me.

Over time, we grew closer, although the anger began to lesson, it never gave me peace. William was not married and never had been. His leadership had come from his uncle who had also been a kindly, wise man. He was humbled to be in my presence and I in his. He had done all he could, to ensure I was comfortable and welcomed into this place. I certainly could never fault him for that.

I was in my early thirties and he was almost fifty. We shared many conversations and advised one another on many things. He asked about my previous life in Atlantis and I either refused, or learnt to change the subject. He knew it had broken my heart to leave and he knew I still struggled with my emotions.

Eventually, he gave up asking about my past and we concentrated on the future. He mentioned that many of the elders in the community had suggested we marry. We were both spiritual and wise, we were both single and he obviously had feelings for me. I had never mentioned Pierre to him, just said that I had been in love once and he had been killed in a freak accident.

William was a good man and I decided that it would be a good way to rekindle my leadership. So, I agreed to marry him, not because I loved him, nor because I fancied him, but for what seemed to be all the wrong reasons. I allowed my remaining emotions to rule me, instead of my heart.

Sometimes we learn how to be, by learning how not to be. Despite knowing that I wasn't in love with this man, I agreed to the marriage. My inner guidance screamed at me to reconsider. In previous times and under different circumstances, I would have listened to nothing less than my soul. Now I would live a lie.

The wedding was arranged very quickly. There was no reason to wait. The elders were pleased and so was everyone else, especially William. I, however, began another dialogue of internal anger towards myself and my lack of integrity.

The Goldfish That Jumped

Soon after our marriage, I became aware that one of the young girls in the court was in love with my husband. I felt her jealousy frequently. She was an angry young lady and was envious of my status. Isabel would openly flirt with William, and on occasions was rude with me.

William often asked me how her behaviour made me feel. I explained that I just dismissed the feelings and ignored her. He certainly had no feelings for her. Neither did he encourage her frequent advances. He merely remained his usual balanced, centred self.

Over the years our friendship grew and I was very fond of William, although I was never in love with him. Intimacy was not easy for me and I battled with myself, day after day. Despite outwardly appearing serene and calm, inside couldn't have been more different. He adored me and I wondered whether or not he knew the truth of my feelings.

I didn't want to love again. It had caused me a whole load of hurt previously. In my eyes, my barriers kept me safe. How wrong I was. How often had I advised others, that barriers only serve to hurt ourselves, by keeping us from the very thing we need the most. What a tangled web we weave.

Years passed and I was introduced to a traveller named Joe who had decided to settle within the community. Our eyes met and the attraction was instant. For the first time in years I was in love again. It was obviously mutual and I was delighted, yet, here I was married to the leader of a huge community.

Despite ignoring my integrity previously, this time I knew I couldn't cross the line and break my marriage vows. William guessed I was in love with the traveller, very soon after we had met. He was always so intuitively connected to me and so loving. Despite his obvious heartache, he offered to renounce the marriage and suggested I elope with Joe.

He said he would offer any, and all, support he could to me, and would even talk with other community leaders, explaining what had happened, asking them to respect our confidentiality, should Joe and I decide to relocate in secrecy. I was touched and deeply grateful.

Here was a man almost broken by his wife's affections for another, yet so profound was his love, that he was willing to allow me to leave, and would even support me in re-establishing myself. I needed to make a decision relating to my future. For the first time in many years, I put my anger aside and went inside myself for the answers.

Finally collecting my thoughts, I went back to the place where I had originally beached on that island. It was somewhere I had never revisited and I meditated. Memories came flooding back of Atlantis. Pierre, those I had missed, lost opportunities and I began to realise that the only person I had really hurt was MYSELF.

Love was the only answer, to every situation that life gives to us on our journey. This was what I taught, yet, it had not been how I had lived, since that last night I had spent with Pierre. William loved me unconditionally and I had deliberately withdrawn from him in so many ways.

I had hoped that he would push me away, so that I could wallow in my emptiness and rage even more. Yet, he never did. Every morning, he awoke with a loving smile and always treated me with such kindness and respect. Tears came easily and soon turned into deep, deep sobbing. All those years of emotion welled up like a volcano.

I don't remember how long I sat rocking and sobbing. My guides drew closer and for the first time in years, the connection with them was as strong as it had always been. I was not berated. Merely welcomed back with open arms and I felt a huge well of love and compassion. My barriers were finally removed, and I felt much lighter, as a deep peace began to envelope me. I slept on the beach that night, knowing where to find shelter, with the welcome assistance of my guides.

William was lying at the side of me when I awoke. As I opened my eyes, I began to say I was sorry. He gently shook his head and covered my lips with his finger. My tears returned and for the very first time, he cried too. We cradled into each others' arms and just rocked perfectly in tune with the other, at long last. How many years had I wasted? How much hurt I had caused him? How much hurt had I caused myself?

Love is so powerful, that it all just seemed to dissolve away into the beach itself. We stayed there for hours, walking and talking. He had brought some provisions and we ate and laughed, just as young lovers do. I felt elated and it was obvious that he did too.

We made love on the beach that day, and it was the most amazing experience I had ever had, up to that point in my life. I realised that was why we call it "making love." I now knew why he had been so very patient with me. He deserved to be the leader, of that there could be no mistake.

The memories of that day will stay with me forever. The powerfulness of the emotions released from the vivid memories of the déjà vu are, to this day, still incredible to experience. Even now, I feel them whilst writing. I have learnt even more from this experience. I can still tangibly feel the power of the unconditional love. The wonder love I received centuries ago from William. How wonderful love truly is.

Later that evening, we arrived, hand in hand, back at the village. We explained that we would be taking a short break from our duties. We would be away travelling for several days. That special time, those precious days we shared, were blissful. We finally cemented our love and friendship.

Upon our return the elders were delighted, as they too, had known eventually I would put down my anger plated armour.

Isabel was completely different with me too. Maybe she sensed that, as we were so in love, nothing would come between us. Maybe it was me that had changed, and, maybe, I no longer attracted that behaviour from her. Whatever, the reason I was grateful.

I began to live again, to teach with more passion and to embrace life. Each and every day held beauty, the smile of a child, walking in the natural surroundings of our beautiful island. I noticed that even the mountains seemed to hold even more magic and were even more colourful.

I guessed I was seeing life through new lenses as my whole perspective had changed. William and I grew closer and closer, as the days became years and I learnt to forgive myself. The more I forgave myself, so the more love I invited in to my whole being.

We lived much longer centuries ago, healing and natural medicines combined with our oneness with nature, made everything in life much simpler and this maintained our health and well-being.

Despite being older than me, William remained in good health for many more years and when, he did eventually pass, (he was aged about 100 years), I too passed over peacefully. It was a soul to soul agreement that we had made years before, there was no reason for one to live without the other. "Just like swans," we had always said: he was my swan and I his swan.

In this lifetime, I met William again. One of the first things he ever said to me was "I love you Mary, totally and unconditionally. There is nothing I wouldn't do for you. My respect for you is profound." We knew we had had past lives together, though it was only several months later that I became aware of the Atlantean connection.

Pierre died in September 2009. I was devastated at the time. He had survived against the odds for so long. It was nothing short of a miracle, that he managed to live so much longer than expected. By coming into my life, he allowed me to bring peace to my soul, I will be forever grateful. Hopefully I brought some peace to his soul too.

I have felt him around me frequently since his passing, and for that too, I have always been grateful. Despite knowing that the soul just changes from the physical being, to the spirit form upon death, and, even though I can see spirits, I still feel the pain of bereavement

By coming into my life, Pierre had allowed me to re-experience the Native American Indian lifetimes. Listening to the native tongue when he and Sam spoke was beautiful to listen to too. Another part of my jigsaw was about to be added.

In February following his death, I did a talk relating to the soul in Lancashire. I met a man called Michael. The instant we meet, we felt the connection and arranged to meet the following weekend. As it always does when you meet a friend from past lives, you pick up where you left off.

We chatted easily, as though we'd known one another forever. We soon experienced the déjà vu that we had been brother and sister in many lifetimes and had been married in other lifetimes. Most were connected to Native American lifetimes and some in Japan.

Michael is a powerful healer and, as such, suggested he did a healing on me. I agreed and it was amazing. The following day, I really struggled to awaken and when I finally did, I was very, very spaced out. As I walked to the bathroom, I felt very different and my skin seemed much darker.

It seemed strange that I was in my nightshirt, rather than dressed as a Native American Indian squaw. As I showered in the hot water, again it seemed odd to me; as I felt I should be under the cold water of a waterfall. The day continued in much the same vein and even my hair seemed much longer, thicker and coarser too.

From that day onwards, my healing abilities gathered an incredible momentum and became much stronger. Michael and I are still great friends. I will always value our connection in this lifetime. I now understand that with the right combination, we are able to bring in our souls parts and become more soulful. Our consciousness expands, as our souls grow.

Nearing Completion

"Logical thinking cannot yield us any knowledge of the empirical world; all knowledge of reality starts from experience and ends in it. Propositions arrived at by purely logical means are completely empty of reality."

Albert Einstein

The name Joseph Elm kept coming up in conversations. He was very well known in spiritual circles. I instinctively knew that I had to meet this man. Last September my friend Amy and, Mr Elm were running a Family Constellation workshop.

These courses had been highly recommended to me and I was looking forward to attending. I would advise anyone and actually EVERYONE to attend one of these workshops. They are incredible – for both male and female, young and old alike. The facilitators ask who has any family issue that they would like to resolve.

They then decide which story is played out. It sounds very simple, and, in its essence it is. However, we ALL experienced the KNOWING of the family members' feelings whoever we were representing once we entered into the circle. The courses are fascinating and inspirational too.

As previously mentioned, I cannot do readings for myself. Nor can I do them for close friends and family. I occasionally get voices of my guides in my head. This particular morning, just as I was about to leave the house, a voice stated very clearly "If you go today, your life will never be the same again."

The Goldfish That Jumped

I knew I had to attend, so replied "Well, I'm going anyway, come Hell or high water. Wish me luck."

We arrived a little early, Joseph introduced himself to us, and I was disappointed to see his energy field was rather dim, and quite small. Usually, spiritual people have large, light brightly coloured energy fields. I had expected to meet a very spiritual man indeed, with a huge light, bright energy field and was quite surprised.

The day unfolded and we thoroughly enjoyed the interaction. Special bonds were made with ALL attendees and we all gained much insight and awareness into family lives. My dear friend James was also on the course, he was picked to play the role of the father-in-law.

Instinctively, I knew that I would be chosen to play his wife. Sure enough I was. Once I stepped into the group circle, I knew James was dead and I was his widow. My button had been pressed AGAIN!!!

He had died very suddenly and I was shocked, bereft and very lonely – I was also capable of standing on my own two feet.... but I didn't want to. It was amazing the innate knowledge of this woman, the insight I had of her life story, that I was so privileged to be playing out. The lady whose story had been chosen, confirmed ALL the details and the information I was both receiving & experiencing.

The tears ran down my cheeks, I was inconsolable, and James – playing the part of a dead man; lay on the floor. The story unfolded and at break I had to leave the group and went outside. I was still crying. Two other members of the group approached me and asked if I wanted someone to come and be with me. Between sobs, I asked for James. Nothing in The Universe is ever coincidence. Instead of my dear friend James, Joe appeared. I was disappointed, but in such a sorry state, that I was just glad to have a hug.

The Goldfish That Jumped

Despite being 5'10", Joseph is several inches taller than me. As soon as he hugged me, just like a wave of electricity, the déjà vu swept through both of us. We both said, at the same time; (me between sobs), that we had done this before and we both knew, at that moment, we had been married in many previous lifetimes. It was quite something and Joe suggested we meet again soon. The sooner, the better. If only I could have known then, what I know now. A series of miracles were about to unfold.

The Goldfish That Jumped

Cae Mabon

*"Wisdom knows what feelings are present
without being lost in them"*

Jack Kornfield.

The following morning, we were both very excited as we spoke on the phone. We agreed to meet in the week. When he arrived, the energy between us was very sensual. We chatted easily and the atmosphere was very charged. It was well past midnight, by the time he got up to leave. It was clear that he wanted to stay. In fact, it would have been very easy to ask him to stay with me that night.

He had made several suggestions that he would have liked to, but, something inside me felt it inappropriate. We hugged several times, indeed it was hard to part, but after a brief kiss, he left in the early hours of the morning. I couldn't get him out of my head.

We continued to speak and/or text daily. The feelings were intensifying daily. The following weekend, he was away for his birthday with his son. At the same time, I was staying in Cae Mabon, a spiritual retreat in Wales. We agreed to meet the following Monday evening.

I wished him "happy birthday" as we spoke over the weekend. I missed him dearly, but something was nagging at me. There is a saying in spiritual circles; "KARMA HURTS, LOVE DOESN'T". The story was about to unfold.

Cae Mabon is a very sacred place, situated in North Wales, near Llanberis, surrounded by mountains. It has a unique peacefulness to it and it touches your soul, profoundly. On the Saturday afternoon, I was sat on a huge boulder in the river, reading Joseph's book. It was interesting and I was captivated; not least because I felt closer to him whilst I read.

I was jolted as the voice of my spirit guide rang through my head, "You have been unfaithful to him." "No I haven't, I wouldn't do that!" was my indignant reply. I was most angry to be accused of something, which I just wouldn't, and couldn't do.

"And…….. you've taken him for granted too." "I wouldn't do that." I venomously replied. "Exactly……... you have done it ALL before and you know the hurt you caused." The realisation hit me hard and I knew this was true.

I began to have thoughts of déjà vu running through me, pictures in my mind of our previous encounters where I had hurt him, SO badly, and caused him, and, our respective families so much pain. WHAT A REVELATION. It smacked hard, and I was very upset and immediately sent as much healing as possible, to the past life situations, and, of course, to Joseph. I asked for release from the karma and the chords were broken.

The situation had been healed. I had accepted responsibility and, as such, when Joe and I meet again, following that weekend, the intensity of the emotions was gone. It was several weeks before I saw him again. Although we enjoyed each other's company, nothing developed further than that.

If I had failed to recognise the karma, the probability of us becoming embroiled in a relationship, one that would have been extremely painful, would, most certainly have happened. He probably would have been unfaithful to me, in order to counteract my unfaithfulness, and probably also taken me for granted too.

My guides had said that my life would change, if I went to the course that day. The bigger picture was about to unfold. Joseph's book was based on a journal he had written, whilst fasting for one week. He had water to drink, basic clothing and bedding but no books, television or reading material. He had no artificial lighting, therefore he would often awake at dawn, sleeping soon after dusk.

Taking time out of everyday life changed him. He became more aware of sounds outside his flat, of looking out at the stars. He also began to take notice of things which he would have previously ignored, or disregarded. Most of all, his intuition became sharper. He became aware of how much we live our lives around a clock, or a watch.

At the official launch of the book, Joe introduced a lady, Elizabeth Gold, who had advised him about nutrition; what foodstuffs to eat prior to fasting, so that he wouldn't have cravings, and also how to reintroduce food afterwards, gently and sensibly. The advice she gave him had indeed worked wonders, he suffered no ill effects during that week. He offered his thanks and she most graciously received it.

Elizabeth is a beautiful petite lady, a most wonderful soul, with blonde curly hair. Her aura shone very brightly indeed, so I knew I would recognize her, if I were to meet her again. In fact, The Universe had already taken care of that particular instance. She was to become a very dear friend. My circle of soul companions was ever increasing, in a most beautiful way and it was about to take a massive leap forward.

The Goldfish That Jumped

Coincidence? - Definitely Not!!

There is no such thing as coincidence

The following week, my dear friend Alison suggested we visit Manchester, to attend the Body, Mind and Spirit fair. I telephoned several friends and we joined the crowds of like-minded people. It was an incredible day; the live music of Tim Wheater, Tai Chi displays, numerous dancers and of course, a variety of lovely stalls selling crystals, jewellery, spiritual books, natural remedies, etc., all aroused our interest.

We all enjoyed it thoroughly. Whilst watching the dancers, I realised I was stood behind Elizabeth. Her blonde curly hair was unmistakable, and, together with her small stature and a huge light coloured energy field, there was no mistaking her. I introduced myself and we chatted, as though we had been friends for years. She stated she wanted a reading, we agreed to meet several days later. The reading was very insightful, helping to explain many issues relevant to her, at that time.

A week later, she telephoned to say she had been delighted with the reading. Some of the issues mentioned in the session, had already occurred. She then asked, if I would consider coming over and giving readings to a party of people. I suggested I could do half-hourly sessions, as long as I had a quiet, private room. Little did I know where this would eventually lead.

At that time, I had no idea that Elizabeth knows just about everyone, who has an interest in spirituality, within the Manchester area. I later found out that she is known as "The Queen of Spiritual Networking."

209

The reading parties had started, these kept me busy throughout the so-called recession. I met many lovely people, from all walks of life. Elizabeth and I became increasingly good friends. She is another person to whom I feel greatly indebted: in a most beautiful and inspirational way.

Each party was superb. I met new people and often we would instantly become great friends. As I had by now progressed quite a way in my spiritual journey, I was able to "know" people I met, whom I had known in past lives. Often, they also had déjà vu of our past lives where we had worked together, trained together, or where I had taught them healing and methods of intuitive awareness.

Every party was amazing in its own way. It was incredible and, as I did the readings for people allowing them to become more aware of their strengths and weaknesses, their karma and life purposes, I too became more aware of mine.

Subsequently, my reputation spread very quickly. One party would lead to another. I would then be invited to other people's homes, to meet their friends and family. Travelling to the parties at various locations, meant I gradually got to know Manchester, more and more.

I was very proud of myself, despite the enormous motorway network. Eventually, I could find my way about without getting lost!!! No mean task, I can assure you! I had always had a phobia of Manchester prior to this point in my life. Having to travel there for work changed that, although, I have not to this day, managed to figure out why this phobia was so strong.

Limitlessness

"I love you, please forgive me, I'm sorry, thank You."

In May 2009, Elizabeth kindly lent me the book "Zero Limits" by Dr. Joe Vitale. I had known that I needed to read the book for several months. I was incredibly grateful. Immediately, upon starting to read the book, things changed much for the better.

The following weekend, I was in The Lakes for the Homeopathy course. It was a beautiful evening and I went to meditate up the mountain. I visualized a villa in Italy: the detail was incredible. The villa was located a few miles outside the nearest village. It was several miles from the nearest town.

It had large entrance gates and was surrounded by lovely trees and delightful, inspirational gardens. Brightly coloured cerise bougainvillea grew around the doorway and smelt heavenly. The house was on three levels and built on a hillside. I entered through the arched doorway into a large hall, with a stairway curling to my right. The wooden floors meant anyone nearby, would be aware of my arrival. There was also a central staircase leading downstairs, to the outdoor pool.

The house was a very unusual shape and design, other rooms where off to the left, including the open-plan kitchen and utility. It was a mixture of many old and new styles, yet so warm and homely. A third set of stairs led down to several bedrooms and bathroom suites. The floors were either wooden or tiled with very few carpets. It was a beautiful place and full of little alcoves, nooks and crannies.

I was aware that it was situated less than an hours' drive from the coast. There was a lake in the distance; either Como or Garda. It was Northern Italy; though not far North. The furniture was mixed, some old, some new, although none matched, it was perfect. The curtains were simple drapes, as the house was not overlooked. It smelt musty though incredibly homely. It was deceptively spacious, the rooms being airy and sparsely furnished.

A lovely swimming pool was to the back of the villa. It overlooked a most beautiful valley of trees and the surrounding mountainside. The vision was breathtaking. It felt very real indeed. I then saw my family around the pool and my youngest grandchild in her child seat. The weather was warm and sunny, though not hot, my sons were cooking on the barbecue.

I was with a man, although I couldn't see his face. I was aware that we were very much in love. We were soul companions, in the truest sense. We laughed and shared so many things in common. We had a deep, most profound respect and understanding of one another.

We had arrived in a lovely silver Mercedes car. As we joined the group, there was much laughter and the smell from the barbeque was delicious. The vision is still very clear in my mind's eye. I do not know yet, what it means. It had all seemed so real, I wondered if I would actually visit this place. Did it exist? As I write this chapter, it really is a pleasure. I often see this beautiful villa in my meditations. I have even invited close friends to stay with us already, should I ever find it!

As I came out of the meditation, I experienced a feeling of completeness in my soul. A joy that was really magical. I had been sat on a huge boulder through the meditation. I had to make sure that I was grounded enough to get down safely. The evening sun was still very warm. The view over Grasmere and Windermere was a wonderful return to reality. It really is such a magical place in The English Lakes.

The Goldfish That Jumped

I felt I had received a lot of energy, from this particularly remote spot. I guessed as I was feeling very hungry, that it was about supper time. I thought I ought to be making tracks home, now that the rush hour traffic had cleared. I was very thirsty too. As I walked down the mountainside, ambling back to my car, I felt a deepening of peace and well-being.

On my way home, I usually call into the petrol station at Largs, before I get onto the motorway. However, for some strange reason that evening, I drove straight past. It was almost as though, the car drove itself into the nearby village of Staveley.

I love this tiny hamlet and knew a local shop would be open somewhere. As I sat on the wall by the river, I was completely in the moment, as I took in the amazing scenery surrounding me. Quite by chance, as dusk approached, I saw a magnificent kingfisher, as it flew over the water.

It was so graceful, elegant, beautiful and amazing too. I was really delighted and touched. They are a very rare bird, appearing to only very few people. Here I was, witnessing this bird in flight over the water, which glistened in the evening sunshine. I did not realize the powerfulness of that evening at the time. The earlier meditation I had done up the mountain, was to prove most significant in the next stage of my life. The kingfisher confirmed that too, although at that time, I had failed to put them together.

The Goldfish That Jumped

Following my Heart and Soul

"Once you make the fundamental choice to be the predominant creative force in your life, any approach you choose to take for your own growth and development can work, and you will be especially attracted to those approaches which will work particularly well for you."

Robert Fritz

May was becoming a magical month for me. I was becoming more and more aware; of both the strength and wisdom of my soul. My guides drew closer to me, their instructions and their advice, was incredibly powerful. My feelings of knowing were growing ever stronger. I was able to listen much more clearly to the directions. I was fully open to allowing The Universe to communicate with me.

That month, the net spread even wider and now I have clients in Cheshire too. Through my dear friend Jenny, one particular lady I had originally met in Manchester, asked me to do a reading party at her house. We agreed the date and I set off for Knutsford.

We had all become great friends and spoke on the telephone regularly. We both agreed there was obviously a past-life connection; because the friendship held such a huge bond instantly. There was a deep knowing between us, which we honoured and trusted. She was very definitely an earth angel, with profound respect for Gaia.

When I arrived, she quickly showed me her garden, which backed on to sacred woodland, I tuned in to the energy, which was very powerful and perfectly balanced. This is very unusual in this day and age. We have come away from our natural roots and connections with nature. She was encouraging all kinds of wildlife into her garden, and, in such a small space, had achieved so much.

My soul was very touched by all the magic, further confirmation, that it would be a superb experience to give readings in this lovely place.

It was indeed, a most beautiful day and I met some very special people. Two ladies at the party have an animal communication business. Both their respective readings were superb. In one of them, I "picked" out a lovely lady and asked Eileen who she was.

"Oh, yes, she's a Homeopathic vet in Yorkshire. She has a wonderful reputation and even teaches Homeopathy in Canada to vets and their staff." "I need to meet her." "Yes, I agree, you would get on very well together, and, no doubt would have a huge connection and lots to talk about," was her prompt reply.

She passed on Syl's number and I called her at the earliest opportunity, several days later. I knew I had to follow this lead and meet Syl. The knowing was so very strong, I knew we must have shared past lives together.

When Syl called me back, I was absolutely delighted. We both felt a huge connection and agreed we should meet, at the earliest possible opportunity. The appointment was duly booked in the diary. I was very excited. I knew our meeting would open doorways, new opportunities and would allow us both to experience further insights into our souls.

Her practise is incredibly busy, thus it would be six weeks before I would meet this special lady. That too was to become very significant in itself.

Meditations

"Mindful attention to any experience is liberating.
Mindfulness brings perspectives, balance and freedom."

Jack Kornfield.

Each week I run a regular meditation evening. Although I guide the group through the meditations, wherever possible, I also partake. More and more frequently, I would see a kingfisher in my meditations; brightly coloured and so beautiful. It was all becoming a little strange, so I called a friend for advice. He laughed, although he was not able to give me any insight.

Later that particular evening, I saw another kingfisher, this time it was massive and as big as the house! I asked other friends what the significance was. Even my dear friend, who is well informed about animal guides, failed to advise me. Thus, I researched myself.

Kingfishers represent all elements, in perfect balance: air, earth, fire and water. They live by the river, fly in the air and their "crimson breast" represents fire. Despite this information, I was still searching. I knew intuitively, that there were more pieces to the jigsaw.

The kingfishers also kept coming up in the readings I gave. Each time, the client would verify what they meant specifically, to them. Even if there was an outstanding significance, relating to the kingfisher in the future, they would call to let me know. It all seemed very odd.

I was advised by my guides to have a kingfisher and a rose, on the front cover of my book. What did it all mean? I was by this point becoming frustrated. I knew there was more. I had learnt that getting frustrated achieves nothing. So, undoubtedly, I was having a lesson in patience!

Whilst in the process of writing this book my daughter and son-in-law celebrated the birth of my second granddaughter. I knew this was a good omen. Within two weeks of her birth I had been invited to meet a friend, in the hope that I would work in her clinic.

Whilst driving to the clinic, I was thinking about the book, hoping that it would be successful in assisting people on their spiritual path. It was a lovely, sunny day. When I arrived, I noticed a poster on the wall, stating that a lady had sold over 600,000 copies of her new book.

Within a few minutes, I was introduced to another lady, who had just had her book accepted by the publishers. Then, on the very same day, when I eventually arrived home, my dear friend invited me for supper. During the conversation, she asked if I had a publisher for my book. I said "no" though I knew The Universe would direct me.

The following evening, which was Sunday, I sent a request to The Universe asking for help in finding a publisher as the book was almost finished.

Three days later, Eileen the animal communicator had an appointment with me. We chatted and she noticed the picture I had done of the kingfisher two years previously. "Who's done that?" she said, "It's marvellous." I explained that I had sketched it, soon after George and I split up. However, it was only several weeks later when I completed it, as the breast was not coloured.

It had been part of my Homeopathy journal for two years, and, as such, had been in a book, closed and unseen. As I now was experiencing weird and wonderful meditations with kingfishers, and, as the birds kept coming up in my readings, I thought I had better frame it, so it was on view in my treatment room.

"Have you got a publisher for your book?" she asked. "No," I replied, "I sent a message to The Universe on Sunday, asking them for their help." "Oh!" she exclaimed......... "when is it you are seeing Syl?" "Next Tuesday - I'm looking forward to it too."

"Did you know her husband was a publisher?"

"No, I had no idea. Really, how wonderful." I replied in dismay!!!

"Yes, do you know what the company is called?"

"No, I don't", I replied as we both turned to look at the picture of the kingfisher.

"FISHER KING PUBLISHING".

I almost fell over – "Are you serious?" I asked, rather dumbly. "Oh yes," she replied and we both laughed and laughed. Nothing in The Universe is ever coincidence. Absolutely nothing.

I travelled up to Yorkshire that Tuesday morning, setting off, soon after dawn. I was so excited and had been unable to sleep the previous night. The journey was straight forward and I passed beautiful countryside, as I travelled further north, into Yorkshire. The sun was rising, I always love this very special time of day. A magical day was about to unfold.

When Syl and I met, we didn't need words or an introduction. The knowing was there and a deep, abiding mutual respect. When I explained about my link with the Kingfisher, we both laughed. "Richard will be in touch," she said.

"Oh, by the way, you need to meet some friends of ours; fellow authors. And, you need to read 'Mystikos'. 'Mystikos' was written by these fellow authors!!!" She left the room and brought me a copy. We promised to keep in touch and we know the bond will strengthen over time.

As I write these closing chapters, I feel a very deep connection to my soul. I have immense gratitude, for all that I have experienced to this current date. How blessed I have been, and, how blessed I am, to have so many friends and wonderful family too.

Going with the flow, being aware of allowing my journey to take me wherever I should go is my goal. I have written the book, in the hope that it touches those who read it, hopefully bringing enjoyment too.

My dearest friend, Andrea stated that she couldn't possibly bare her soul so openly, and admired me for doing so. I AM THAT I AM. Nothing more, nothing less. I have written this book purely from the heart. My hope is that it has touched, on some level at least, YOUR HEART AND SOUL.

I hope the book is successful, in that, my desire is that many, many people, at some point in their lives, are able to relate to my writing. The Buddhists teach that we are ALL ONE. There is NO SEPARATION. As we grow spiritually, so in turn, we help others to grow. My life, to date, has been a very rich tapestry of experiences, and, I am truly grateful for all that I have experienced; both the joyous and the painful.

As I picked the plums from the tree in my garden last autumn, with each one I collected thoughts of gratitude. Gratitude to all those who have helped and supported me on my journey. My life is very fruitful now, and I take one day as it comes. I no longer have attachments or expectations in life. Whatever comes, comes, I shall embrace it. I am happier than I have ever been in my life, a contentment that runs deep within.

Glastonbury and Chalice Well

"There are only two ways to live your life.
One is as though nothing is a miracle.
The other is as though everything is a miracle."

Albert Einstein

My friend Serena has become very dear, we both teach subjects relating to spirituality. Indeed, we are very busy ladies, most weekends we are teaching/working or on courses, increasing our awareness. In September, 2010, she requested a reading, feeling that she wanted clarity on a couple of issues in her life.

In the reading, I could "see" her enjoying Chalice Well gardens and also walking in Glastonbury town centre. I also "knew" she had a voucher, someone had won a holiday. After the reading, she explained that she had wanted to visit the area for some time, though she had no-one to go with. Her parents had won a voucher, for two people to stay at the Hilton hotel. It was valid for use in the local area around Newbury.

Glastonbury was a place I had wanted to visit, for some time. In spring 2010, a friend asked if I would accompany him to stay and visit the area. I declined, knowing in my soul that, at that time, it would not have been right. I also knew I would visit later in the year.

Without hesitation, I suggested that I accompany her. It felt right and I was in no doubt whatsoever that it would be a wonderful trip. It would give us time to get to know one another better too. She stated that she was free on the weekend of 25 - 27th September, so was I.

It was incredible, certainly no coincidence; which we both recognised. The hotel was duly booked, we were both excited. I knew it was to be a remarkable short break for us both. I also knew it would change our lives.

She arrived to pick me up, early that September morning. We set off in glorious, bright autumn sunshine. We laughed and joked and whilst we stopped at the services, I purchased a CD set of Love songs, to keep us company on our adventure. We were like Thelma and Louise!

Several miles outside Bath, I recall saying to Serena that the trip would change us profoundly. Life would never be the same again for either of us, obviously in a good way. I explained that she would find the love of her life very soon, and, that it was to be a very speedy romance. They would both know it was right. They belonged together.

The journey was easy and traffic reasonable, until, that is, we neared Bath. We were stuck in a traffic jam for two hours!!! We chatted and laughed, wondering what the delay was. Eventually, we parked the car, making our way to the shops and restaurants, for some lunch. We stated that no doubt, it would become clear why we had been delayed. We both expected that the reason for the delay related to Bath. However, this wasn't the case, as we were to find out later that evening.

Bath is a most beautiful city, the architecture is stunning, it is so magnificent and we were both inspired by its beauty. Serena had recently purchased a new camera, she was happy clicking for hours, as we admired the scenery. We walked through the beautiful park, watching the canal barges, gently move below us from the bridge. We pottered through church yards and found wonderful, quaint shops. A major highlight, was of course, sampling the delicious products, namely cakes and home-made breads!

Eventually, daylight was fading, we knew that it was time to make our way to the hotel, at Newbury. The countryside was so lovely. As we travelled, through numerous villages and towns, past lovely unspoilt countryside and valleys we felt the powerfulness of the whole area. Serena feels energies in a similar way to me, we both became aware, especially, when we passed through ley lines.

Whilst planning our trip, we had noted the white horses on the map. We decided to join the dots, as it were. We were amazed to note, that they made an inverted triangle. As we passed through each one of these lines, our heart centres were expanded. It really was an incredible sensation, each time it happened.

Passing the white horse on the main road, (theA4), was a really powerful experience. We were both close to tears, simply with the volume of the emotion. The daylight was replaced by that of the moon, which was in its full glory. We felt that it almost led us to the hotel. By now, we were quite tired and ready to freshen up. We found the Hilton easily and quickly grabbed our luggage. We were shattered and ready for a cuppa and a rest.

As we walked through the double doors to the room, we heard someone singing behind us. "Nothing in The Universe is by chance ladies, I am here to open the door for you." We stared at each other. One thing about the spiritually aware, is that we don't wear a label. In fact, many feel isolated and keep their spirituality to themselves. So, here we were, with someone whom we had just met, and that was the opening statement!!! No coincidence indeed.

He introduced himself as Jeremy and asked if we were staying. We answered "Yes," and he invited us to sit with him by the piano later, explaining that he too was going to freshen up and would be with us soon....... So, no surprises for guessing what we did after a quick cuppa and a shower!

Fully rejuvenated and looking gorgeous, we made our way to the hotel foyer, to meet Jeremy again. Serena and I do not drink, neither were we hungry, so, if he hadn't have been there at exactly that time, we would never have ventured from our hotel room. The timing was so precise, that it was definitely all meant to be.

"We Are Sailing", by Rod Stewart, was the introductory piece of the man playing on the piano. He explained that he played it in memory of a dear friend he had lost. As I smiled at him, I thought of my cousin Alex, who is still so very sadly missed. Alex too had been a musician. I thought how lovely it is to honour someone's memory, especially musically.

Jeremy continued to play and we thoroughly enjoyed ourselves. Chatting and enjoying live music was a wonderful combination. Whilst we listened, we were all sharing stories relating to spirituality. The bond was made and it was lovely. As I left for bed that night, I passed Jeremy my card and asked him to keep in touch..... he duly gave me his contact details too and wished me goodnight.

The following morning I knew I had to contact him. I texted to say we were still in the hotel and would love to meet up and say "Thank You" and "Au Revoir". He replied immediately, suggesting that he would meet us in the dining area.

I was well aware there was a powerful connection between us. We chatted and we all agreed that it was as if we had known each other before. As we were all aware of our past lives, we agreed without hesitation, that this was fate. For whatever reason, we were meant to meet again.

Jeremy had an engagement to attend, later that day and thus had to leave. He asked if either of us were ever in London, to contact him and that we would meet again. I explained that I was due to be in London within two weeks. He was delighted and suggested I let him know the arrangements.

Glastonbury is said to be the heart centre of the world. Serena and I did much healing that weekend in the locality and we felt that by being there, our heart centres were also touched and opened further. It was an altogether wonderful experience and one that we both treasure to this day.

I had mentioned to her that we would both be changed forever. Within a month, I had introduced her to my dear friend Daniel. Within a short space of time they began dating, were engaged within six weeks, and they plan to marry in February 2011.

Meanwhile, Jeremy and I kept in touch daily. My mother is a huge Cliff Richard fan, she had asked me to attend his concert with her at The Royal Albert Hall, in October. Her friend Zara was also on the coach trip; another Cliff fan.

The arrangements were all made, and I contacted Jeremy with the details. He agreed to meet us at the hotel. I was so excited to be seeing him again and willed the coach driver to drive faster. Within a few minutes of our arrival, he was there. We hugged and hugged for ages, whilst people watched from the coach! The delight at our reunion was massive for each of us.

Three guests were meant to depart with us from Preston. They did not show at the designated time. I knew now, why, they had not come to watch the show. Obviously, there were three spare tickets, so, very luckily, I had managed to get Jeremy a ticket to attend the show too. The miracles had been happening all day. By now I knew that The Universe had a bigger plan for us.

He quickly freshened up in the hotel room, and we travelled into London for the performance. Although I had a ticket for the show, my ticket had been booked at the same time as had my mother's so that we would be sat together. Zara had a single ticket sat a few seats away. Jeremy's ticket was at the opposite side of the theatre!

The Goldfish That Jumped

The Royal Albert Hall holds 5,000 people in the audience. The show was a sell-out, so was fully booked. Mum was beginning to panic. I calmly asked The Universe for help and assured her, all would be well. "You won't be sat together, you know." She was clearly agitated. I assured her once again, suggesting that she and Zara take the two tickets, ensuring they were sat together. Jeremy and I would sort ourselves out and we would meet them inside later.

It had been a very long day. We had been up since about 5am to travel by coach into London. I realised I was hungry, so Jeremy and I agreed to try to quickly find somewhere to eat, right in the centre of the capital.

We knew we only had a few minutes and rushed down the road to a fast food outlet. Throughout the meal I requested divine assistance, *if* it was for our Highest Good. We both agreed that we would not attend the show if we were to be separated. We would rather just go for a drink in a local bar, then meet up with the coach party later.

When we arrived at The Royal Albert Hall, we were only about 10 minutes late and the show had begun already. We stood, hand in hand, in the entrance and explained that our travel company had made a mistake with our tickets, and, obviously we needed to be together. "I'm very, very sorry, the theatre is fully booked and we have no vacancies. I am unable to help you." Jeremy and I just looked at each other and said "Please could you have another look?" She called her manager and within a few seconds we were shown into a box.

We couldn't believe our luck. The Universe really treated us with utmost kindness. The box was lovely and spacious. We hugged and sang along with Cliff. The hall was absolutely full. What a miracle! The view was tremendous and the show amazing. Cliff is a wonderful performer and we really, thoroughly enjoyed ourselves.

The Goldfish That Jumped

Despite looking for mum and Zara, there were too many people and we were unable to locate them. Although we hadn't seen any familiar faces, we had been spotted by two ladies who were sat opposite us on the coach. Following the show we all met up again to be taken back to the hotel.

As we got back on the coach, everyone was buzzing. Mum was of course, wondering what had happened. "Well, did you get in then?" "Yes, we got a box seat."...... "You never did, you're joking!" She was flabbergasted. "Yeah, we did," and we both nodded, whilst grinning from ear to ear. She was not impressed. "You jammy buggers," she said, "it's me that likes Cliff anyways."

It was hilarious and everyone around us on the coach was laughing at mum's facial expressions. She still wasn't sure whether or not we were telling the truth, when the ladies across from us stated that they had seen us in the box. Mum roared laughing and it has been a huge joke since that day.

The Goldfish That Jumped

Hawaiian Huna Healing

Effectiveness is the measure of truth

Hawaiian proverb

Jeremy and I had really enjoyed ourselves and we kept in touch for several weeks after that night. However, despite saying he was coming to Lancashire, nothing materialised. I began to suspect that there was karma involved and, it would soon become clear, exactly what the karma related to.

One Saturday evening, I was making my supper in the kitchen when, without any warning, I experienced the most excruciating pain in my heart centre. In my minds' eye, I received a picture of Jeremy and I as a married couple in an Egyptian past life. I was made aware that he had been unfaithful, many, many times and I had pleaded with him to stop. His behaviour continued for years whilst I pretended everything was okay. The most important thing I learnt from that lifetime, was that I allowed myself to become his victim, lying to myself at the same time.

Even worse than that, I became embittered with the events, blaming Jeremy for everything. The pain worsened very quickly, I was doubled over. I texted three friends for help, explaining I was in a lot of pain. My friend Gary immediately replied, asking what was happening. We spoke on the phone and he sent healing. Within seconds his three Hawaiian guides surrounded me, forming a triangle. Within moments I was coughing, choking, then trying to be sick.

Then, just as Gary's voice was telling me, the pain began to dissolve, dissipate and disappear. A little at first, and then more, until it was utterly and completely gone! It was a miracle and I was incredibly grateful!

So powerful was that experience, that I attended his Huna healing workshop several weeks later. This again has increased my healing and personal power. The readings have been even more amazing and even more detailed too.

Gary and I had been friends for months through the internet social friendship site 'Facebook'. Looking back to the initial time I joined the site, he was one of the first people I added to my friends list. We connected on Facebook regularly for several weeks. He was a friend of Elizabeth Gold, so I knew he would be a great contact and was probably very soulful.

Looking through his profile he seemed to have very similar principles to me. He taught through love and forgiveness, in a very similar way to the healings listed in the "Zero Limits" book. He also had a keen interest in healing and Isis, as well as Mary Magdalene. I always work from my intuition. It had clearly guided me to add him.

We chatted for months on "Facebook" then began to email one another. He mentioned that he was doing an evening workshop in Manchester, in October. I was thrilled, as I had known in my soul that we were meant to meet. It is funny how we perceive people, without having met them before. He was shorter than I thought and his voice didn't seem to match his personality.

The evening workshop was amazingly energising and full of really simple but powerful healings, and did exactly what it said on the tin, as they say. Plus I met some really inspirational people. I signed up for the weekend workshop that evening, knowing in my soul that it was the right thing to do. Since that time, the awakenings and energies I have experienced, have been nothing short of truly miraculous.

The Goldfish That Jumped

As you may remember, from being a very small child I have had a major phobia of worms. There was nothing that my parents could remember that had happened to me that would explain this unreasonable behaviour I displayed.

When I saw a worm I had always been frightened they would kill me! It was very confusing and made no sense to any logic-minded person.

In February 2008, I had followed my instinct and attended a workshop relating to Emotional Freedom Technique. (E.F.T.) I have had an interest in alternative medicine and therapies for many years. This particular one had caught my attention.

The workshop was held locally and I attended with several friends. That afternoon the facilitator asked for a volunteer. I explained that I had had this phobia all my life and it was impossible to explain. She chose me as her guinea pig and I agreed. Little did I know what lay ahead, as the picture was about to unfold.

E.F.T. is highly effective in removing phobias and unwanted behaviours. By tapping on various acupressure points on the body, such as the hand, and the head, whilst it dissolves. She asked me to rank the problem on a scale of one to ten, ten being the worst, how strong the problem is.

"Thirty!" I replied and my flesh was creeping, I could feel terror and blind panic filling me from within, and it got stronger and stronger as she was about to start the process. She then said that a worm had crawled up the stairs and was right next to my foot. I wanted to just get away, anywhere, to run from this overwhelming fear. She stayed calm and helped me not to run whilst we tapped.

I was mesmerised and horrified by the worms, especially the deep red worms and also became extremely agitated by their movements. She proceeded to tap the acupressure points and eventually, after much tapping, we slowly got the fear down to my panic-stricken 'thirty' to a more manageable count of three.

To be successful, it needs to be a zero count, in order that the therapist knows it has completely disappeared, and resolution obtained. Despite trying many different methods, the count failed to reduce from three.

So, she began again, and this time asked me to visualize that a worm had crawled up the stairs, and was ON MY FOOT, TOUCHING MY SKIN. I immediately had an extreme, emotional reaction.

I was instantly consumed with panic, started shaking uncontrollably and I was struggling to breathe. Huge tears ran down my cheeks. "Where are you?" she asked, "you are perfectly safe and you can stop this at anytime and come back into the room." I certainly didn't feel that I could stop the process that had started.

Absolute terror consumed my whole being. "Where are you?" she repeated. Slowly, and with a very unsteady voice, I replied "I'm in a dungeon. I'm hooked onto the wall and now it's my turn to be tortured, before I die." "Where is your pain?" she asked. "In my kidneys, they've just thumped me with a rod and punched me."

My back was incredibly painful indeed. I was still crying, shaking and struggling to breathe, especially with the pain in my ribs and kidney region. "Who is with you?" "There are seven others with me, they will be tortured first." I knew that as part of my punishment, I was made to listen to their screams as they were mutilated, before being murdered. It was agony, on all levels mentally, physically, emotionally and spiritually.

Now my turn had come, I too was about to be tortured. I clearly recalled that as I had been unhooked, my right knee had hit the floor and the worms and slugs were wriggling amongst the straw. Therefore, my only recollection of the whole scenario was the worms. That's why I had always thought that if they touched me, they would kill me. The power of the unconscious mind really is incredible.

We must have managed some tapping, as I do recall that the count reduced to one and a half. However, I cannot recall the further tapping at all. I was unable to reduce the count to zero, and she agreed that, as the whole process had been traumatic and exhausting, we should quit for the day. I was in so much shock and my back was incredibly painful. I wandered around the gardens of the beautiful college for the rest of the afternoon, too dazed and shocked to partake in any other activities.

When I arrived home, my son knew something was wrong and questioned me relating to the day's events. As I relayed what had happened, he was very surprised. The children had always known of my fear and, apparently one day had put worms in my bed, thinking it would be funny. I have no recollection of this at all, though they said I ran from the bedroom, down the stairs in hysteria! They stated that it had taken almost an hour to calm me. To be honest, up to that point, they had all thought it was a huge joke.

As I told my son what had happened, he could see that I was still in pain in the kidney region of my back. He suggested he take a look. When I lifted my jumper, he could see that I was covered in deep bruises, around that area. It was black and blue. I had been taking the homeopathic remedy arnica, since I got home for the shock anyway, now I increased the dose to assist the bruises to heal too.

Over the coming days, the bruises faded and the shock dissipated. However, I was still aware that pieces of this jigsaw were missing, and that I needed more clarity, in order to put this fear to bed, once and for all. I could recall the pictures and had seen the faces of those who were murdered alongside me.

One of them I knew to be Daniel, soon to be Serena's husband, another was a friend from the coast, my close friends Dennis, Charles, Rupert, Harry and others whom I had recently met. I knew that it would be difficult to put them all together though managed to introduce Dennis to Rupert. We were attending a talk one night, relating to the crystal skulls. I had never mentioned to any of them their past life connection, and thus, when they met, they had no idea of my insights.

The instant they met, they agreed they knew one another. Then Dennis stated, "You were pushed down the stone stairs backwards, before being murdered." Rupert was amazed. It was their first meeting and their first conversation. "How the hell did you know that?" Rupert was clearly shocked, "Because I was there with you."

When you become aware of your soul, these meetings happen frequently and this was certainly a wonderful meeting. Rupert shared that he had recently been experiencing much déjà vu relating to this time and, like me, had sent the healing to all concerned. I explained my part in all of this and we accepted what had happened.

I am blessed to know many powerful healers and asked my dear friend Thomas to help me to lay this to rest. He promptly agreed, and I stated that I would love to be able to walk on the grass outside, without footwear, after the session. By using hypnotherapy and combinations of Neuro Linguistic Programming, we uncovered differing aspects of the jigsaw.

It certainly wasn't just about being murdered in the dungeon. I had been chased by others and different aspects of the much bigger picture unfolded. The room began to fill with light beings. Thomas is also sensitive to energies/spirits etc., and we both felt them in the room. We thought they had come to celebrate my letting go of the fear.

Suddenly, I became aware I was back in Atlantis, and many ascended Masters had been trapped in a wormhole; a vortex of time. I released them and felt their joy. What a day. Two hours later, for the first time in my life, I walked barefoot outside on the grass. I was delighted. It had been quite an achievement.

The Goldfish That Jumped

I will be forever grateful for Thomas's help that day. I honestly thought that was closure. How wrong we can be sometimes! Sometimes we think we have cleared something completely, when all we have done is to clear one layer of the onion, which comes back around for our attention at some later point.

I have been teaching Reiki for several years now and love this particular aspect of my work. One particular Saturday in February 2010, I was teaching with Serena and Libby, both Reiki Masters, who wanted to see how I taught Reiki as I hadn't taught them levels One & Two. Thus, they had come along to watch me teach Reiki One.

When we heal someone, we move down the body, from the head to the feet, balancing energies as we go. Wherever there has been past life trauma, it is usual for the injury/markings to reappear, then disappear within a few days. Sometimes, the person being healed has an awareness of that particular past life or "knows" what is happening through the treatment. An example would be where noose-line markings appear on the throat when someone has been hung in previous lifetimes.

It is not uncommon for people to have had feelings of suffocation that the doctors cannot explain. Neither is it uncommon for people to say that they feel they have been beheaded, strangled or hung in past lives. Subsequently, they are unable to wear anything tight around their necks.

Most people who are unaware, or who are only just re-awakening, struggle to comprehend this fact. Thus, as a teacher, I feel it relevant to make them aware that this is always a possibility of healing. Many of my patients have received healing and have experienced past life déjà vu around a particular area of the body that has previously given them a great deal of pain. They will often "see" a sword wound and have felt that the pain, when present, feels like they have been stabbed.

For me, it has happened far too often for me to disregard. So, this particular day, whilst I was teaching, I recounted my story relating to the worm phobia. I explained that following the E.F.T. I had severe bruising on my back. The words had literally just left my mouth, when I was aware that again, I was in agony in that region of my back. It was all I could do to stand up. I quickly asked both Libby and Serena to come into my treatment room and remove this agonizing pain. They confirmed the area was black and blue, on both left and right sides.

I again took several doses of arnica and magnesium phosphate to treat the pain and the deep bruising. The girls checked my back which was still black and blue, several hours later. I sent healing and tuned into the pain, although it was not clear why it had happened again, almost two years later.

The day continued and although the bruising remained, I continued teaching. The students were all amazed when I showed them my back. A living example! When the students had all gone home, I chatted with Serena to see if she had any further insights. I explained that I had identified all those I was murdered with and had sent healing. I had also sent to the dungeon itself, as buildings also take on energy and pain. I had recognised the person who had tortured us and again sent healing and forgiveness. Surely, I hadn't left any stones unturned? She and I had no further answers, and so, I had to accept that for the time being at least, that was that.

Serena and I had arranged to do some Mother Earth healing together. Our friendship was deepening and we were thrilled to spend time together doing what we love. Several days before we met my back was sore again and bruised. This time the bruising was deeper and even more painful too, especially when I turned. Just before we set off for Alderley Edge in Cheshire, she checked my bruises and was most surprised. We sent healing and were both, at that time, rather surprised that no further insights came to mind.

It proved to be a wonderful day and a very beautiful part of the country. I had never been there before and the views were spectacular. We found a lovely pub for lunch and chatted about life, our experiences, we both discussed that we both felt we were ready to welcome new relationships in our lives. Little did we know how quickly these new life stories would unfold for us both.

As you can see throughout the book, I had always wanted a relationship that would be fulfilling, loving, productive and of course needed someone who understood my work and my abilities. This man would have to be very special indeed as I was no longer willing to compromise. I hoped too that he would be a healer. Having travelled a long way on my inner journey, I knew I needed someone who was also well into their own soulful journey. In January 2010 I met someone to whom I was instantly attracted. He too was quite far down the spiritual path. Would we ever come together? Each time I saw him I had a deep inner knowing. Would my prayers be answered?

The Universe, as always had a bigger plan. I still had inner work to do and more healing was required for my personal growth and understanding. The story would further unfold. None of us like to be given lessons in patience. However, the best things in life are worth waiting for.

Two days later, my friend Neil invited me to his boat. We had been friends for almost a year and I was fond of him. We had always got on well together and I was looking forward to spending time with him. The weather was very windy, so we decided to walk rather than sail. Whilst walking, we chatted and laughed. Then as I twisted, in order to get through a gate, I said "Ouch," as I felt the pain in my back. He asked what the matter was and I explained the whole story.

As a fellow hypnotherapist, he agreed to hypnotise me and to try to uncover the rest of the story. I was very reluctant and actually felt fearful. I explained that during the E.F.T. I had reacted very strongly, and he agreed he would keep me safe, as we worked through the hypnotherapy. I really wasn't sure what to do, he agreed that it was my decision, and he would support me either way. Several minutes passed, before I eventually agreed to be hypnotised.

As soon as he began, I was in the dungeon again. I was terrified and crying. He continued and eventually, though not an easy experience for me, I gathered a few more of the jigsaw pieces together.

Neil and I had been married. We were the leaders of a community of very spiritual people, rather like the Cathars, Gnostics or Essenes. I suppose it is rather like the Chinese and the Tibetans nowadays, or the Jews and the Nazis. Although he wanted children, I refused, as I felt it unfair as our peoples were often ousted out of the main community.

We often lived in hiding, rather than being allowed to integrate freely with others. We were aware of the whereabouts of the other communities similar to ourselves and we often heard stories of how the leaders' children were captured and used as pawns in a game of blackmail, in order to gather information which might lead to the locations of other communities.

Huge ransoms were paid to people who knew of our whereabouts, so we could be sought out. The masses believed what they were told: that we were practising magic and were very nasty people. Fear consumed them.

Actually we were very peaceful people, using healing abilities and being aware of energies just as the ancient Atlanteans had been. This is very similar to the Native American Indians and Aborigines too.

The story began to unfold. We lived on an island. I am not quite sure which one, although it was in Europe. We always travelled in darkness, as it provided cover for us. As our instincts were sharpened, we were able to cover great distances easily. Often Neil would liaise with the other communities and was frequently away. I was a powerful clairvoyant, as I am now, and he always ordered a protector to be with me at all times.

This particular night, I knew something was wrong. We had argued again about children, but my decision was final. He left, though I begged him not to go. The pictures were very clear. The emotions were also very real and powerful. Once he had reached the mainland, after crossing the water, he was attacked and murdered swiftly. They knew of our location and at dawn the community was raided. The pictures ended there. I knew we were all murdered, though I had no further detail. I sent healing to both him and myself. I explained his part in the scene. Quite an amazing coincidence that he should be the one to hypnotise me!

Despite knowing that most of the picture was now available to me, I knew intuitively, that more would follow. . .

In November 2010 I felt really drawn to go on Gary's Hawaiian Huna healing weekend. I had yet another great time, with lots of fabulous energies pouring into me, and old heavy ones leaving me forever. More importantly, I discovered that Gary was a life coach and business coach, helping people to achieve their goals and fulfil their destiny. I knew I wanted my book to be finished, but something was holding me back, I had a block that I could not access or clear myself, and I knew intuitively that with all the Huna, NLP and other tools at his disposal he would be better equipped than most coaches to help me, so we made arrangements for me to have a private consultation with him.

I felt a huge knowing with this man and a huge trust too. I knew there was something about the worm phobia that was still to be uncovered, and I knew that this was holding me back from achieving my life's purpose, whatever that might be. I needed someone I could trust and someone who was also a powerful healer, although I had no clue at this point that the book and the worms may somehow be connected!

The appointment was booked for Friday morning. On that day, I was awakened at 4am by my spirit guides. There was such an excitement in the air, I struggled to get back off to sleep. Two hours later, I was still awake, so made a cuppa and read, whilst I sat in bed. My guides were very close to me and stated that this day would change things for the better; for the rest of my life.

My guides were with me in the car, as I drove south. It was bitterly cold and I arrived that wintry morning in thick fog. It was really quite mystical. Gary was pleased to see me and following a cup of tea, we got to work. His guides had already told him that intuitive ways of working would reveal more than the more usual psychology based questions.

We began by discussing how I was blocking myself and I explained that a deeply bad feeling arose within me, and I would find other things to do.

Gary shared with me a Hawaiian technique to keep me totally safe whilst allowing me to follow the bad feeling to its root cause, where I could gain the learnings and teachings I would need to allow the feelings to go away. By flying way up high, he made me fly many millions of miles above the earth, in order to keep me safe, and yet still get the inner learnings I needed. These learnings were deeply personal to me so I will not share them, but I can share the rest of the past life déjà vu....

The story unravelled itself like a ball of barbed wire. I returned to the dungeon once more. The final jigsaw pieces were about to be fitted together, once and for all. As the leaders' wife, I was the last to be murdered. It had been decided that as part of my punishment, that I should bear witness to all of our peoples being mutilated and murdered before me.

The women and children were first. My captors promised that I would be spared, if I gave them the localities of the other communes. I knew that if I had done, we would be murdered anyway, thus was not about to divulge any information at all.

It was a grotesque scene. The screams, the blood, the mutilated body parts all lay at my feet. I was hung onto the wall, several feet above the floor and the weight of my body making me extremely uncomfortable, which also made breathing difficult. I connected to Source and stayed in my heart centre, as, one by one, my peoples were killed. I couldn't understand where Neil was and hoped he was safe.

The previous night as I begged him not to leave, I asked my bodyguard to stay close to him. Neil had spotted him and had ordered him to return to my side. By the time he had arrived in the morning, it was too late. Through a gap in the tiny window I saw Jeremy. The expression of horror on his face was something that I can still recollect now. I communicated with him, through extra sensory perception to leave and hide in a local cave. He knew the whereabouts of the other communities, so could join them later.

During the E.F.T. my initial memory was of myself with seven male companions. I now came to realise that these were our Consulate of advisors. They in turn were murdered. I held that connection to the Divine even more so. Then, it was my turn. Just before I was unhooked from the wall, I was punched in my back.

The severity of the beating caused me to lose my concentration and I lost my connection with Source. My soul returned with a jolt, into my body. I looked below to see the worms wriggling amongst the mutilated bodies. I felt awful as I watched the worms and, as they resembled the nerves and tendons of the bodies so closely, I thought; in my deluded state, that the bodies might surely come back to life!

Once unhooked from my chains on the wall, I stumbled as I was dragged forward to my doom, and as I did so my right knee hit the floor which was covered with bright red worms. Hardly any wonder that I had always assumed that being near red worms would kill me!

All of a sudden I realised, the connection between the worms and not finishing the book, or indeed anything that might raise my profile above that of an everyday hard worker!

As part of the learnings I received from deep within my ancestry, family-DNA, past life, or call it what you will, I discovered that we were all held in the prison for teaching sacred spiritual lessons that contradicted The Church, and personally

241

empowering people which the Government did not want. And it was my writings that had led them to us, for which I felt deeply guilty. Funnily enough I felt far more guilt for the deaths and torture of my friends than I did for my own nasty brutal end. And even more for the deaths of my people. Our whole community was wiped out. Jeremy was the only one who survived.

So here I am in this lifetime, self-sabotaging myself from making writings or other teachings public, because very deep down, my inner self was terrified of repeating the whole terrifying horrific episode!

At last the jigsaw is complete. I have the whole picture now. Or at least, I think so.....

And then Gary brought me back to ordinary reality, and we shared our thoughts and experiences, because I had been 'out of it' and in deep trance during the whole episode, and very grateful to have finally cleared so much away.

Less than 48 hours later, I awoke at 3am. I did not feel like I needed anything, and yet I was drawn to walk into the kitchen. I am often without footwear, so am mindful where I walk. There before me was a long, red worm. My sons were in bed, so I had no option other than to pick it up with a tissue and remove it. I realised that my heart rate had not increased, that I wasn't shaking either. This was very unusual. I gathered up the said worm, it began to wriggle. Still I remained calm. I actually spoke to it and said I would place it outside the door, as it did not belong in my home and sent it some healing. It was quite surreal. The worm phobia was no more.

The following morning, I promptly texted Gary to inform him of this miracle, which had happened at 3am. In his usual witty manner, he replied "so, it's true then, the early bird really does catch the worm!"

Music

"Music is the mediator between the
spiritual and the sensual life"

Ludwig Van Beethoven

Music lifts the soul. I love singing and always joined the
choir as a youngster. Singing elevates and feeds the soul and
the expression of song is one of the fastest ways in which to
recover from a gloomy day or situation. I love attending live
music and opera, orchestras and groups. In fact it really is a
passion of mine to experience or listen to live music and I
encourage clients and patients to listen and to partake in music
regularly, even if it is just bopping to the radio in the kitchen.

We recently attended a concert with Deva Primal and
Miten with Manose in Gorton Monastery in Manchester. It
was awesome and after one particular chant to encourage
for positive change, the energy wave was so powerful that
it set off the fire alarms! Many people in the audience felt it
pass to the back of the building and out into the surrounding
area. Buddhist chanting can clear all negative energies.
There are numerous examples of Buddhist monks who have
cleared polluted areas and lakes by chanting. The Earth holds
memories of pain and obviously the concentration camps in
Germany were very congested with negative, heavy, dense
energy. Healers over the last few decades have cleared much of
that pain.

The Goldfish That Jumped

The Present Present

"Those who are forever watchful, who study themselves day and night, and who wholly strive for nirvana, all their passions pass away"

Dalai Lama

The year after I left George, I lived each day as if it was my last. I learned to be in the moment, in the present, right here, right now. In that year, I did all the remaining things I had desired, and "knew" I had to do. Without desire, expectation or attachments, I now go with the flow, living from moment to moment, trusting in divine providence and love.

Blessed with many friends I am open to opportunities and challenges as and when they arrive. I live through my soul, my intuition and guidance from Source. I love spending time with friends & family. Gary has helped me tremendously and I am forever grateful. Friendships last through lifetimes and we often find one another again.

This book has finally materialised into reality through our collaboration, with lots of new students and connections (especially through Facebook, thank you Mr Zuckerberg). I have had even more amazing healings, new clients, more abundance in all things positive which is pouring through as I clear out my 'stuff' and literally en-light-en.

I absolutely had to go through the absolutely yin dark suicidal punishing times, in order to swing back out into the yang light, and to allow myself to be me, the flowing energy of both light and dark, accepting both as being me.

And I tell you this so you can know that you can do this too. In fact, anyone can do this too once you open up to your own infinite possibilities, to love yourself *first*. As they say on airline flight safety briefings before you take off, 'please fit your own oxygen mask *before* helping other people with theirs'.

Where in your life can you allow you to love yourself more? I'm not just talking about a little me-time, or self-pampering, I'm talking about allowing you to be you, allowing time to be, and not to beat yourself up in your head like we have all been taught to do. Until now. Now you can allow things to just be as they are without judgement. What other people do is just what other people do. What you do with that is your stuff. So you can let it go, and just…. be.

And to repeat a catch phrase of mine "what other people think about you, is actually nothing to do with you!!!"

How different is that to most people's way of thinking? Constantly criticising, moaning, judging, blaming, and otherwise getting their knickers in a knot about what other people get up to.

I went to hell and back to find this deeply profound learning, and I give it to you here, because I don't want you to have to go there too. It was deeply unpleasant. I was swimming round and round in my dark stagnant goldfish bowl.

Until, that is, I found forgiveness and finally, I was the Goldfish that Jumped! Forgiveness for me; first and foremost. And then I found it deeply releasing to simply just accept myself. To allow me some slack and let go of all those little nasty voices in my head giving me a hard time.

I realised that they weren't even my voices, they belonged to the negative-thought-trained-humanity, that eventually became my parents, aunts, uncles, teachers, 'friends' and others who bullied, cajoled, pushed and pulled me this way and that, not allowing my own true free spirit to fly free and just BE!

By becoming gentle with myself, I found a really important person. I found me.

And the last thing I did, while down in the deepest darkest despair, was to realise I had nowhere further to go. I had reached rock bottom and found enough was enough. Only I could change my life, the way I viewed myself, the way I criticised myself.

I learned from books like this one, that there are alternatives, and the only person who can change me, is me. And you can too.

I am now living my life whole-*heart*edly.

When people first meet me, they say I have the ability to accept them as they are. Little do they know, I was once just like them, and I have learned over time to be accepting.

So now I can let go of the past and welcome a new brighter future of my own choosing, because the best way to know the future is to create it for yourself mindfully.

I would like to travel around Italy, Sicily and to revisit Samos. I have since had frequent déjà vu regarding Egypt and the Goddess Isis. I would love to visit Egypt this year, for whatever reason I am not yet sure, perhaps I will experience more déjà vu, or perhaps I just have a deep knowing that I need to be there. I know that I will return, sooner, rather than later.

Derwentwater is a beautiful location. There is a house right by the lakeside, which I have visualised as my own, for several years. Waking up in the Lakes, a place which really opens and empowers my soul is one of the most wonderful things I choose to experience. To enjoy this magical setting, each and every day would be precious. Being awakened by the sound of birdsong in the mornings, the absolute quietness, and stillness of the lake and all its beauty would be very welcoming.

Who knows maybe I will write more books from there too, looking out at the moon and the clear vibrant sparkling stars, hearing the night birdsong, the sounds of nature doing its own thing, without man's interference. Looking into the lakeside waters sprinkled with jewels that reflect in the moonlight of the goddess.

I love frosty mornings, the cold air, the sense of awe and majesty. I love the rain, even when it is really heavy. There is something magical about being caught in a rain storm. Derwentwater is such a wonderful place, I am sure it would continually inspire my soul on its journey. I realise that in the winter months The Lakes are subject to harsher weather, though I really don't mind this at all. Even if it became impossible to get out in severe weather such as deep snow, all would be well.

At last I have found an inner peace. It has taken me a long time to get here, but, it has all been worthwhile. I constantly enjoy my family and friends, especially my beautiful granddaughters. My work gives me immense pleasure, touching peoples' souls so that they may recognize their own souls' desires and find fulfilment in their lives. As I said in the introduction, I sincerely hope this book has held your hand lovingly. Maybe it has inspired you, given you hope during your dark nights of the soul.

Go forward with love, light and the freedom of your soul. Listen to your intuition and embrace the JOY life brings at every given opportunity; from the flowering of a rose in your garden, to the smile of someone you love. Enjoy music and laughter, friends and family, wherever you may be, and, as you enjoy the feeling of inner joyfulness may you in turn spread that to others.......

Smell you later!

Mary xxx

..Alice laughed. "There's no use trying," she said: "one can't believe impossible things." "I daresay you haven't had much practice," said the Queen. "When I was your age, I always did it for half-an-hour a day. Why, sometimes I've believed as many as six impossible things before breakfast."...

Through the Looking Glass, L. Carroll

The Goldfish That Jumped

Bibliography

Zero Limits	Dr Joe Vitale & Dr Hew Ihaleakala Len
Eat, Love, Pray	Elizabeth Gilbert
Pilgrims Guide & Journal	Glastonbury Edition
The Prophet	Kahlil Gibran
Bag of Jewels	Susan Hayward & Malcolm Cohan
The Little Book of Instructions	Robert Frederick Ltd.
The Wise Heart	Jack Kornfield
A Return to Love	Marianne Williamson
A Little Light on the Spiritual Laws	Diana Cooper
The Boy Who Saw True	Cyril Scott
The Living Matrix	Greg Becker & Harry Massey

The Goldfish That Jumped

The Goldfish That Jumped

The Goldfish That Jumped

Author Information

Mary runs a busy healing practice and is available for private consultations, group sessions and public speaking.

You can contact her through her websites.

www. journeyintoyoursoul.com

or

www.marypsychichealer.co.uk

and her FaceBook pages

www.facebook.com/journeyintoyoursoul

or

www.facebook.com/thegoldfishthatjumped

She is currently working on her next book and details will be featured on the website in due course.

Ever hopeful that you find success and fulfilment in life.

The Goldfish That Jumped

Merchandise

Mary has recently produced a wide variety of meditation/relaxation recordings & CD's.

Titles include:

"Down To The Beach"

"The Rose"

"The Log Cabin"

They encourage you to open your heart and inspire your soul.

These are available through her websites

www. journeyintoyoursoul.com

or

www.marypsychichealer.co.uk

You can contact her through
the above websites
and her FaceBook pages

www.facebook.com/journeyintoyoursoul

and

www.facebook.com/thegoldfishthatjumped

The Goldfish That Jumped

The Goldfish That Jumped

Lightning Source UK Ltd.
Milton Keynes UK
UKOW04f0902010813

214705UK00010B/166/P